i

DO

die in obedience

to

CHRIST

RAYMOND CULLEN

I Do (Die in Obedience) to Christ
Copyright © 2019
Author: Raymond Cullen
Email: raycullen58@hotmail.com

Cover design: Anointed Fire™ House
Publisher: Anointed Fire™ House
Publisher's Website: www.anointedfirehouse.com

ISBN: 978-1-7331127-1-0

Disclaimer: This book is designed to provide information and motivation to our readers. It is sold with the understanding that the publisher is not engaged to render any type of psychological, legal, or any other kind of professional advice. No warranties or guarantees are expressed or implied by the author, since every man has his own measure of faith. The individual author(s) shall

Acknowledgments

Thanks be to God the Father, Jesus, the Son
and the precious Holy Spirit who are the actual
authors and finishers of this work.
To my wife of 42 years, Charmaine Deanne,
who has also been my sister, friend, spiritual
adviser, lover, accountability partner, life
coach and help meet. What a woman!!!
To my children, Kendrea Tamara, CharRae
Deanne Michael Adrian, Tiffany Danyell and
Raymond C. III (Tray), who loved me with all of
my inconsistencies while trying to find myself
throughout the various phases of my life.
To my many grandchildren who have only
witnessed the born-again life of G-Daddy.
Thank you, Lord!

To my Father, Raymond C. Cullen Sr. May he
rest in Him who gave me my life, my name and
an opportunity to choose abundant life in
Christ.

To my Darling Mother, Rev. Mildred Aletha
Huff, who never stopped praying and believing

in me, probably due to her relationship with Christ and her recognizing His abiding in me, even when I couldn't see. No matter how low I went, she never gave up on me. Whenever I was wrong, she immediately let me know, but she never ever let me go. That's My Mama!

To my six siblings, Evelyn Mildred, Barbara June, Clem Michael, Ruby Ellen, Spring Sylvia and Charlene Renee, who never stopped supporting whatever God was doing in your youngest brother's life.

To Pastor Ronald and 1st Lady Sandy Lassiter and the Regeneration Outreach Christian Center of Newport News, VA. for accepting, covering, and loving me just as I am.

To my Spiritual Fathers the late Bishop Nate Holcomb of the Christian House of Prayer in Killeen, TX. and Dr. Tony Evans of Oak Cliff Bible Fellowship in Dallas, TX., who have both taught me and are still teaching me kingdom principles that honor God and His people.

To Bishop Felton Hawkins who, for 20 years, poured into me a constant message of God's love that produced salvation, deliverance, humility, accountability, repentance and maturity. He and Pastor Terrance Johnson played a key role in my transformation from a carnal man to a Kingdom Man.

To Dr. William R. Harvey, my colleagues, faculty, staff, alumni, parents and students of Hampton University for allowing me to grow gracefully, yet still play a role in mentoring and producing so many great men and women throughout this world.

To all my spiritual sons and daughters coming from here, there and everywhere who were born to my wife and I "not by power, nor by might but by My Spirit, saith the Lord of hosts"! You know exactly who you are!

And finally, to my spiritual daughters, Louise Nunga and Tiffany Buckner who were determined to see this God-ordained work come into fruition, whether I thought I was ready or not. DETERMINED indeed!

Thank you all for the roles you have played in my life and I want you to know that I love each and every one of you with an **Eros love** (of course to Charmaine only), **Storge love** to my family and **Philia love** to my friends and associates, all leading to **Agape love in Christ Jesus.** - Raymond C. Cullen Jr.

Table of Contents

Introduction

To me, the term "I DO" is actually an acronym for "I Die in ObeDIEnce." There is only one true way to demonstrate obedience, and that is to die of myself (my way, my ideas, my wants, and my desires). Just as **1 Samuel 15:22** tells us, **"To obey is better than sacrifice, and to hearken than the fat of rams."** If I do not die of myself, I can do what I am told and still not be obedient. So, what I do then becomes a sacrifice, and what I accomplish will never be the best possible, because I'm not giving all that I have. I'm just doing what you instructed me to do to get what I want. So, I'm making a sacrifice from what I really want in order to try to accomplish what you want, but if I die to what I want, I make myself usable for what God wants. So, He gets the glory. This means if He wants me to be obedient to whomever or whatever, I can do so with joy because I've already dismissed the mindset if I can't have it my way, then I don't want it no way at all. Why is this true? Because I have now died of feeling that my way is the only way.

Look at the word "OBEDIENCE" and you will see the answer to this dilemma. Right in the center of "ObeDIEnce" is the word "DIE". In the center of the word "DIE" is the word "I". Thus, I DIE in ObeDIEnce. You can never separate the need to die from ObeDIEnce. As you can plainly see, the word DIE is in the center of ObeDIEnce. In God's Kingdom, dying is the centerfold of ObeDIEnce. In fact, dying is the centerfold to Kingdom living! If we do not die in ObeDIEnce, we will die because of disobeDIEnce. Jesus demonstrated this principle as stated in **Hebrews 5:8-9, "Though He were a Son, yet He learned obedience by the things which He suffered; And being made perfect, He became the author of eternal salvation unto all them that obey Him."** Therefore, His learning obedience became the gateway for us to *obtain* eternal salvation, while our learning obedience is what allows us to *maintain* eternal salvation.

Just as in **1 Samuel 3:1-18**, the young lad named Samuel was taught the various responsibilities of ministering in the temple by his spiritual father, Eli, yet **verse 7** plainly states, **"Now Samuel did not yet know the**

Lord, neither was the Word of the Lord yet revealed unto him." He did, however, know how to assist with the ministry, but when God actually called him three times, he responded to the authority he was used to being obedient to. Eli had to allow him to go through the process of learning God's voice, and once confirmed, he instructed him on how to respond to God's calling. He didn't teach himself, but he learned obedience by being obedient. As he learned to recognize the voice of God, he learned to be obedient to God's instructions.

This is why I say, "I DO ObeDIEnce, or to be more speclflc, I Die in ObeDIEnce to CHRIST."
Pastor Raymond C. Cullen, Jr.

Chapter 1

Just Say, "I Do, Lord!"

I was delivered from cursing, promiscuity, drugs, beer and cigarettes. I grew up in Vineland, New Jersey. My father left us when I was about six-years old. Then came my stepfather, who was very kind, but had a drinking problem. His alcoholism revealed a personality that led me to vow never to drink when I grew up, but that seed had already been planted. This is because, even as youngsters, we were allowed to "share" a beer once in a while if we begged hard enough. Keep in mind that we went to church regularly! Our mother made sure that my six siblings and I not only were in attendance, but we also were key participants. We all knew the Ten Commandments, the 23rd Psalm, the Beatitudes, the Lord's Prayer, and the names of all the books of the Bible by heart, but my stepfather would never come with us.

When I was seventeen, I accepted Jesus as my Savior and was told I had to "tarry" for the Holy Ghost, so I did. For a solid week, I gave my all, and while I was "tarrying", it seemed that everyone was receiving Him except me. For this reason, I came to the conclusion that I had committed too many sins as a young boy to receive forgiveness. I figured, "If I'm going to Hell, I might as well start the fire now." I ended up in worse condition than my stepfather and my father. I began to chase (and catch) girls and older women. I began abusing any and every kind of drug or alcohol I could get my hands on. The things I did would make your head spin. Yet, I thought I was a "nice" person, but obviously, I had become a victim of a generational curse. I had the Deliverer walking with me, but I wasn't walking with Him. Despite hearing God speak through various men and women concerning the call on my life, the older I got, the more impossible those prophecies seemed. That's because the older I got, the more sin I got into. Truly, sin does separate us from the love of God. He never stops loving us, but we definitely find it harder to love Him and ourselves. Even though I had confessed Jesus and believed in Him, I was lacking the washing and regeneration of the Word. Thanks to God's grace and mercy, He never left me, nor did He forsake me.

Throughout all of this, God blessed me with a woman (actually a girl). She was twelve and I was fourteen when we first started going together. By the time we got married, she was sixteen with two children. She has been there for me from that point to this point, though there were times when I did everything possible to abuse her both mentally and physically. I finally came to the place when I was tired of the fast life, but more importantly, I realized I was burning my gifts and talents full force, while losing my life, wife and family at the same time. Throughout all of this time of living in sin, my mother never stopped praying for us and consistently pointed us to the cross of Christ.

I was a finance and accounting travel supervisor in the U.S. Army, lead singer in a busy R&B band, and a disc jockey, traveling regularly throughout three European countries. All this, along with getting high on beer, hard liquor, expensive and cheap wines, "speed", cocaine, "crack", "acid", marijuana, hashish, opium, "uppers", "downers", heroin and tobacco. I did this almost daily for at least twelve years! I'm sure you can imagine the stories that went along with all of that drug abuse. All I can say is that I know I should be dead and gone.

Once I surrendered and cried out to God about how tired I was, He said to me that He would go with me through recovery, but "recovery" had to be done His way. I agreed. The very next thing I distinctly heard Him say was, "You're going to prison. Now, turn yourself in." At that point, I became as Saul of Tarsus, knocked off my high horse. I felt blinded, not able to see what I was getting into, but I trusted Him. By faith, He allowed me to experience the "I DO Process". I literally had to die in ObeDIEnce to Christ and I learned to live in ObeDIEnce to Christ. He not only brought me through, but He is still bringing me through. During my ten months in prison, He worked so many miracles that by the time I was released, I was convinced that He was still calling me, dirty ears and all.

I was paroled in January 1988; I was without employment, diagnosed with diabetes in February 1988 and yet, still dabbling in drugs, beer and church. Finally, in May 1992, I answered the call to preach, and through the Word of God, I was delivered from cursing, drugs, beer, cigarettes and chasing loose women. I knew I had, and still have, a long way to go, but I've learned that God's Word is true, and He confirms this with the following signs. He saved my marriage. (Thank you, Lord, for my beautiful wife, Charmaine!) He also saved all four of our children: Kendrea, CharRae, Tiffany and Raymond III (Tray), who were destined to become alcoholics, potheads or crackheads. We dedicated them all back to Christ years ago, while attempting to let our lights shine before them. Then, He revealed another son, Michael, who also loves the Lord and was 36 years old when we met, with a wife and three children. Of course, by the grace of God, we immediately accepted them all into the family. And at the present time, my wife and I have been blessed with 17 grandchildren who all address us as G-Daddy and Ganny, along with a plethora of spiritual sons and daughters from around the world. Hallelujah! The devil once tried to convince me that I was a cursed man, but God nailed the curse to the cross and Jesus paid the cost! Guess what? He did it for you too. So, what are you going to do? Just say, "I DO, Lord!" or "I Die in ObeDIEnce to CHRIST!"

Chapter 2

She Said, "I Do" To The Man First

"I Found Myself In An Abortion Clinic"
by Charmaine D. Cullen

I was raised up as a "daddy's girl." When I was about seven years old, my dad and mother separated, and it hurt me to the core. My dad left town and began to go from state to state. Every now and then, he would show up again in New Jersey, where my mother and I lived. This would give me the hope of my parents getting back together, but that never happened.

Don't get me wrong, although I was a "daddy's girl," I loved my mother dearly. After dad was gone, she did all she could do to raise me up in the church. When I turned twelve, my dad returned again to New Jersey and settled down for a while. He found himself a girlfriend. I still wanted my parents back together, but I must admit that my daddy's girlfriend was nice to me. When I made weekend visits, I went to church with her on Sundays.

The first Sunday I went with her to church, I met Ray, who is now my husband of forty-two years. A friend of his once told me that the minute Ray saw me come in, he placed a claim on my life, saying that I was going to be his wife. (Mind you, I was twelve and he was fourteen at the time. As the old folks would say, we were still wet behind the ears.) In the beginning, I didn't want anything to do with him, but as time went by, he won me over.

I was always mature for my age because I spent a lot of time with older people. While hanging out with my dad, at twelve years of age, I began to smoke pot with him. (Ray, who was, at that time, my boyfriend, says that I turned him on to it as well.) By the time I reached fourteen, I got pregnant and we had a daughter (Kendrea). This really made me think I was grown, so I continued drinking alcohol, partying even more and breaking my mother's heart. Still, she stuck by me, and she (along with Ray and his family) helped me all they could with our daughter.

Do you know that when you're sneaking around and being rebellious, it catches up with you? The devil set a trap for me, and guess what? I fell right into it. I got pregnant again!

This time, my mother threw her hands up, as if to say, "Lord, you deal with her. I don't know what else to do." By now, my dad had left his girlfriend and moved to another state. Ray signed up to go into the military to provide for his children without revealing me to the military, which had laws about illegitimate children. A month before leaving, he went with me on a doctor's appointment, and then, we went to the recruiter's office. After leaving that office, he asked me a question that made my heart melt, "Charmaine, will you marry me?" I couldn't wait to ask my mother if I could marry him. I had put her through so much that she said, "I think this is the best thing to do." At age sixteen, I got married and had our second daughter (CharRae).

Ray's first duty assignment was overseas in Germany. The party was on then, and my house became the party house. We began to tap into stronger drugs; you name it, and we did it.

Ray and I started to have marital problems. We would love each other one day and fight like cats and dogs the next. (Sometimes, I would even start the fight because I felt I could hold my own!) While in Germany, we had another daughter (Tiffany), and our marriage continued to fall apart. We left Germany and came back to the States, continuing to party hearty—and fight. We even separated a couple of times, but found ourselves back together, still doing our own things. After about three years in the States, we ended up back overseas; this time, in Holland, The Netherlands. This is when I discovered that I was pregnant with our fourth child and only son (Tray). I was twenty-three years old with four children. Once I arrived in Holland, I really lost my mind. Satan had me sure enough. I was doing things I thought I would never do. I found myself in a relationship with another man, looking to fill a void that could only be filled by the Lord Himself. You know, what's done in the dark surely comes to light. I found out that I was pregnant again; this time, it wasn't Ray's baby. Satan really set me up and was sitting back laughing at me. (You know this is how he works.) I found myself in an abortion clinic, doing something I said I would never do. I had to go to my husband and confess, and then, ask for forgiveness.

God began to tug on my heart. I began to dislike myself and almost couldn't stand to look at myself in the mirror. Even when I was doing my dirt, I'd always ask God for forgiveness. After this, I'd turn around and do the same thing, but I eventually came to the end of my rope. I told God, "Lord, I've tried everything I thought I was bad enough to try, and now, Lord, I'm ready to try You." I invited Jesus into my heart, and He delivered me from drugs and alcohol, smoking and wanting to cheat on my husband. Instantly, He began to put my marriage back together and much better than before. I truly believe all of this restoration has manifested because Ray and I accepted the forgiveness Jesus Christ offers to all, and then, we demonstrated that forgiveness to each other and so many others. It's a daily demonstration, but I'm a witness that He's a keeper. Yes, He is! I finally said, "I DO" to the Lover and Savior of my soul, Jesus Christ, and He saved my marriage, my family and my life! So, you can plainly see that it really does matter who you say I DO to, and if you make Christ your first choice, He'll back you up, according to the Father's choice! I finally got it right. I DO... I Die in ObeDIEnce to Christ!

Chapter 3

Happy New Life

Forget about New Year's Resolutions, let's strive for new life resolutions. Resolutions are "the acts or results of resolving something. The thing determined regarding a future action." Restitution is "gaining back something that has been lost or taken away; a reimbursement or restoration." Resolutions are based on hope for future results, while restitution comes immediately from God, based on proper positioning in Christ. In other words, if we're in Christ, yet struggling with a stubborn habit or sin, God restores our liberty by giving us His Word. Like the Israelites of the Old Testament, our flesh will want to go back to the way things were, even if it's not in accordance with the promises of God. "**Therefore, if any man be in Christ, he is a new creature: old things are passed away, all things are become new" (2 Corinthians 5:17).** Since we are new creatures in Christ, we need to celebrate a life of new habits and bury the old in the same manner that we take time to celebrate the New Year.

First of all, there are good habits and bad habits, but we must understand that habits are a part of life. They can have a positive or negative effect on the way we live. A habit is a custom, a thing done often, and hence, easily. It's a usual way of doing something; this is what leads to an addiction. It is a disposition or involuntary tendency to act constantly in a certain manner, usually an acquired frequent repetition. Beloved, as believers, we need to change those bad habits into good habits or, I should say, "God habits". Please keep in mind the fact that everything good is not always God, but God is always good! For example, if God showed you that a brother or sister is to become your prospective marriage partner, it would seem like a good idea to test the product in advance (you know, "try it before you buy it"), especially when you consider the divorce and separation statistics of today. I mean, it only seems proper to share your love in advance with the one you're destined to share your life with, right? Wrong! God's idea of a sexual relationship is reserved for a man and a woman who He has joined together in Holy Matrimony. All other replicas are definitely fraudulent **(Matthew 19:3-9).** On the other hand, you may already be married and get angry with your spouse for some reason and decide that it's alright to withhold sex as a punishment to express your anger. After all, it's your body, isn't it? Once again, this may seem like a good idea, but God says it's a no-no. His good idea suggests that your body belongs to your spouse. Therefore, we are only to defraud each other upon agreement with one another and in this case for the specific purpose of fasting and prayer **(1 Corinthians 7:5).**

For a comparison of how the people of God become complacent in bondage, even after being delivered, let's evaluate **Exodus 14:11-14. "And they said unto Moses, because there were no graves in Egypt, hast thou taken us away to die in the wilderness? Wherefore hast thou dealt with us, to carry us forth out of Egypt? Is not this the word that we did tell thee in Egypt, saying, Let us alone, that we may serve the Egyptians? For it had been better for us to serve the Egyptians, than that we should die in the wilderness. And Moses said unto the people, fear ye not, stand still,**

and see the salvation of the Lord, which he
will show to you today, for the Egyptians
whom ye have seen today, ye shall see them
again no more forever. The Lord shall fight for
you, and ye shall hold your peace." Here, we
can see that our flesh is going to hurt when we
deny it of what it has become accustomed to.
Like the Israelites of the Old Testament, our
flesh will want to go back to the way things
were, even if it's not in accordance with the
promises of God. So, to obtain our deliverance,
we must hear the Word of the Lord—**Fear not,
stand still and see the salvation of the Lord.** To
"stand still" does not mean to do nothing at all;
it means to wait on the Lord. To wait on the
Lord is to serve the Lord. Just listen to **Isaiah's**
words in **chapter 40, verse 31** of his book. It
reads, **"But they that wait upon the Lord shall
renew their strength; they shall mount up
with wings as eagles; they shall run, and not
be weary; and shall walk and not faint."** I
don't believe he meant for us to wait and do
nothing, because the rewards from the waiting
are all results from working out. For instance,
renewed strength comes from some sort of

workout. To mount up, to run, and even to walk are all physical abilities that are maintained by constant application. This means that waiting on or serving the Lord must become a habit.

Instead of waiting on the Lord, the Israelites made a habit of murmuring, complaining and constantly disobeying and disappointing God. Many times, we too are guilty of becoming complacent with bad habits, such as negative speaking, broken promises, tardiness, drinking, smoking, poor money management, drug abuse, or overeating, just to name a few. All of these habits may or may not be sins, but they are weights because they hinder our divine destinies to serve God in one way or another. **"Wherefore seeing we also are compassed about with so great a cloud of witnesses, let us lay aside every weight, and the sin which doth so easily beset us, and let us run with patience the race that is set before us, looking unto Jesus the author and finisher of our faith; who for the joy that was set before him endured the cross, despising the shame, and is**

set down at the right hand of the throne of God" (Hebrews 12:1-2). Let's lose the dead WEIGHT while we WAIT to ESCALATE to higher heights in CHRIST! **"And Moses said unto the people, fear ye not, stand still, and see the salvation of the Lord, which he will show to you today: for the Egyptians whom ye have seen today, ye shall see them again no more forever. The Lord shall fight for you, and ye shall hold your peace" (Exodus 14:15).** You just say, I DO and watch Him do what He said He'll do!

Chapter 4

What Must I Give Up?

Do I have to give up drinking alcohol, partying, cigarettes, dancing, movies, sexual intercourse, immodest dress, unsaved friends, bad language, gambling, etc.? Tell me, preacher. Tell me, teacher. Tell me, talk show host. Tell me, role model. Tell me, parents. What must I give up? As new Christians in the Kingdom of God, I know this question is on the top of your list of concerns, as it relates to becoming the vessels of honor that God has called you to be. How do I know? I know because this issue is not settled with a great number of Christians who have been saved for years. One of the main reasons is because of the fear of the word "SACRIFICE". My prayer is that through this chapter, your fear of sacrifice will become your faith in sacrifice.

Let's start out by defining the words "Christian" and "sacrifice. A Christian is: a follower or adherent of Jesus Christ. The word "adherent" means to stick to something or to cling. "Sacrifice" means the act of offering or to give up something. Therefore, a "Christian sacrifice" is actually when a follower of Jesus Christ is giving up something. Thus, the question still remains, "What must I give up?" In **Hebrews 10:10-14,** the author explains that by God's will, we are sanctified once and for all because Jesus Christ offered His body for us. The word "sanctified" means to be set apart. We are set apart as a chosen generation so that we will show forth the praises of Him who hath called us out of darkness into His marvelous light **(1 Peter 2:9).** Hallelujah! No other sacrifice will ever take away sins. So, as we study God's Word daily and pray, the Holy Spirit begins to reveal certain areas in our lives that are not pleasing to God. Don't take it to mean that you have to sacrifice it. **"But this man, after he had offered one sacrifice for sins forever, sat down on the right hand of God: From hence forth expecting till his enemies be made His footstool" (Hebrews 10:12-13).** This is how we turn the fear of sacrifice into faith in sacrifice, and this is what salvation is based on—the sacrifice Jesus made for you and me at Calvary. This is why faith is so important because, as **Hebrews 11:6** states, **"Without faith it is impossible to please Him; for he that cometh**

to God must believe that he is and that he is a rewarder of them that diligently seek Him." So again, you ask, "What must I give up?" Well, Jesus gives the answer in **Matthew 9:23**. He said, **"If any man will come after me, let him deny himself and take up his cross daily and follow me."** The Apostle Paul admonishes us in **Romans 12:1 to present our bodies as a living sacrifice, holy and acceptable unto God, which is our reasonable service.** In other words, don't try to make a sacrifice; we are called to become a sacrifice. Always remember, **"Obedience is better than sacrifice" (1 Samuel 15:22).**

To be more specific, we must give up living in sin. The Apostle Paul instructs us in **Romans 6:12-15, "Let not sin therefore reign in your mortal body, that ye should obey it in the lusts thereof. Neither yield ye your members as instruments of unrighteousness unto sin: but yield yourselves unto God, as those that are alive from the dead, and your members as instruments of righteousness unto God. For sin shall not have dominion over you: for ye**

27

are not under the law, but under grace. What then? Shall we sin, because we are not under the law, but under grace? God forbid."

Just Die in ObeDIEnce to Christ!

Chapter 5

To Believe or Not to Believe

To believe or not to believe? That is the question. Ask yourself, "Then, what must I believe? Can I believe without faith? Or more importantly, what exactly is faith?" The answer to all of these questions support the words that Jesus spoke in **Mark 16:16,** which are really plain and simple—**believe and be baptized and you shall be saved; believe not and you shall be damned.** Upon understanding this, it seems fitting that we establish what we should believe. To start off, let's take a look at **Romans 10:9, "That if thou shalt confess with thy mouth the Lord Jesus and believe in thy heart that God hath raised him from the dead, thou shalt be saved."** Paul tells us to believe that God has raised Jesus Christ from the dead, but he also tells us to confess Jesus Christ as the Lord of our lives and to speak this confession with our mouths. To believe is not enough. The Bible tells us **"Thou believest that there is one God; thou doest well: the devils also believe, and tremble. But wilt thou know, O vain man, that faith without works is dead" (James 2:19-20)? James 2:19** confirms that we cannot possibly believe without faith, because believing is a type of works, as explained in **James 2:20, "Faith without works is dead."** Then, Paul reminds us, **"For by grace are ye saved through faith, and that not of yourselves: It is the gift of God; not of works, lest any man should boast" (Ephesians 2:8-9).** So, we are saved by God's grace through faith in His Son, the Lord, Jesus Christ. Many people have problems with this scripture because they can't understand how this mere man, this great prophet (as they say) could possibly be our Savior or, first and foremost, even our God. This is why we must have faith. You see, it was not man's instruction or command to worship Jesus as Lord. It was and still is God's idea. **"Let God be true and every man a liar" (Romans 3:4)**.

Have you ever noticed that many other religions or cults want to believe God in part, rather than completely? What I am saying is that God without Jesus is incomplete, God without His Spirit is incomplete, and Jesus without the Holy Spirit is incomplete. The Holy Spirit without God or the Son is incomplete.

32

But if it takes faith in this Gospel message for us to live victorious lives for God's glory, we must have a solid foundation on which to build our faith. That foundation is the Word of God, the Holy Scriptures—The Holy Bible. We must come to the conclusion that God's Word is true, and even though He uses mere men and women to bring forth His message of eternal life, we must remember that **"all scripture is given by inspiration of God" (2 Timothy 3:16).** Scripture was birthed by the Holy Spirit of God. We have to rely wholly on God's Word, which is Jesus Christ Himself **(John 1:1-14).** As a result, we will become holy in God's Word. A brother once told me, "If you live by half of the Word, you end up with "wo", as in "Woe unto you, hypocrites!" **Matthew 23:23-28** sheds light on how the Lord feels about hypocrites. It reads, **"Woe unto you, scribes and Pharisees, hypocrites! For ye pay tithe of mint and anise and cummin, and have omitted the weightier matters of the law, judgment, mercy, and faith: these ought ye to have done, and not to leave the other undone. Ye blind guides, which strain at a gnat, and swallow a camel.**

Woe unto you, scribes, and Pharisees, hypocrites! For ye make clean the outside of the cup and of the platter, but within they are full of extortion and excess. Thou blind Pharisee, cleanse first that which is within the cup and platter, that the outside of them may be clean also. Woe unto you, scribes and Pharisees, hypocrites! For ye are like unto whited sepulchres, which indeed appear beautiful outward, but are within full of dead men's bones, and of all uncleanness. Even so ye also outwardly appear righteous unto men, but within you are full of hypocrisy and iniquity." Let's stop right here because in the following verses, Jesus continues to express His displeasure towards hypocrisy and how it affects the advancement of the Kingdom of God. Woe unto you, hypocrites!

The Apostle Paul wants to teach us how to believe and avoid hypocrisy. He begins with three thought-provoking questions.

"How then shall they call on him in whom they have not yet believed? And how shall

**they believe in him of whom they have not
heard? And how shall they hear without a
preacher? So then faith cometh by hearing,
and hearing by the Word of God" (Romans
10:14, 17).**

What is this "faith" that we so cordially speak
of? It is imperative that new converts focus on
obtaining a working knowledge of the biblical
definition of faith: **"Now faith is the substance
of things hoped for, the evidence of things not
seen" (Hebrews 11:1).** I don't believe that any
man can fully interpret this scripture to present
the entire definition of what is encased in the
word "faith". I say this because God is
constantly showing me different revelations of
what faith is and where it can take us. For
instance, we learn from the Bible that God has
given every man a certain measure of faith
(**Romans 12:3**). A person may have "weak
faith" as mentioned in **Romans 4:19**, which
reads, **"And being not weak in faith, he
considered not his own body now dead, when
he was about an hundred years old, neither
yet the deadness of Sarah's womb."** This

"weak faith" would have hindered the birth of Abraham's son, Isaac, if he'd been bound by it. I call it "baby" or "new convert faith", but it's still faith.

A person may have "little faith", which Jesus spoke of in **Matthew 8:26, "And he saith unto them, why are ye fearful, O ye of little faith? Then he arose and rebuked the winds and the sea; there was a great calm." In verse 25**, the disciples cried out saying**, "Lord save us."** Their display of "little faith" was them not recognizing the fact that salvation was aboard the ship, along with them. Does the disciples' reaction sound familiar? Of course, it does! At some point, we have all allowed our surrounding circumstances to cause us to lose focus of our salvation. Losing our focus will cause us to walk in "little faith". New converts can expect to walk in little faith but must be determined to mature to the level of faith that God will have them to obtain for His glory.

Next, there is a "growing faith" that Paul speaks about in **2 Thessalonians 1:3**. It reads,

"We are bound to thank God always for you, brethren, as it is meet, because that your faith groweth exceedingly, and the charity of every one of you all toward each other aboundeth." Here, the apostle is sharing with the members of the church how he and the other leaders thank God for their "growing faith"—a faith that resulted in their continuously growing love for one another. This is the same testimony that our pastors will share with us as we exercise "growing faith".

Finally, in **Romans 4:20-21**, the Word says about Abraham that **"He staggered not at the promise of God through unbelief; but was strong in faith, giving glory to God; and being fully persuaded that, what he had promised, he was able to perform." This is an example of "strong faith".** Abraham would not give in to what the circumstances that surrounded him were indicating, but he decided to believe and receive what God said. A key point to acknowledge here is that he gave glory to God. We also must learn to give God the glory at all times. When the praises of God are going up, the blessings of God start coming down.

Jesus spoke of "great faith" in the story of the centurion. **"When Jesus heard it, he marveled and said to them that followed him, verily I say unto you, I have not found so great faith, no, not in Israel" (Matthew 8:10)**. In reading the entire text of **Matthew 8:5-13**, the story shows that Jesus marveled at the "great faith" of the centurion because the soldier knew that he was not worthy of Jesus visiting his home (knowing that Jesus was called to the house of Israel). Yet, he had faith enough to believe that Jesus could simply speak healing and the Word would travel to his house and heal his servant. **Verse 13** tells us, "**And the servant was healed in the selfsame hour."** When we learn to read and digest God's Word, and begin to walk in the will and promises of God with confidence, knowing that Jesus is in Heaven sitting at the right hand of God, our Father, interceding for us, yet living within us at the same time ,we can then say we have "great faith". **"Thy word**

is a lamp unto my feet, and a light unto my path" (Psalms 119:105).

Jesus spoke of "mustard seed faith". **"And Jesus said unto them, because of your unbelief: For verily I say unto you If you have faith as a grain of mustard seed, ye shall say unto the mountains, remove to yonder place; and it shall move; and nothing shall be impossible to you" (Matthew 17:20).** What Jesus is saying is that faith begins from a tiny seed that eventually will grow to "mountain-moving faith", whereas, nothing shall be impossible for you. The key to the growth process in faith lies within the ground that the faith seed is sown. The seed must be sown in "good" ground, and God is the root of all good. Our faith has to originate from and must be attached to God's purposes and destiny for our lives.

So, how do we sow faith seeds into good ground? Again, the Word of God says, **"So then faith cometh by hearing, and hearing by the Word of God" (Romans 10:17).** Our faith grows as we hear God's Word preached through ministers sent by Him and anointed by the Holy Spirit.

I encourage you to study your Bible diligently. New Christians should not try to explain to unbelievers how their faith works, because they are not yet prepared to give a full and thorough explanation. What they can do is tell whoever wants to challenge their faith to try Jesus themselves, beginning with mustard seed faith, which may look like weak faith or, better yet, little faith—an evidence of growing faith, leading to strong faith, resulting in great faith, which will produce mountain-moving faith! I DO! Now, what are you gonna do?

Chapter 6

God's Choice of Servants

Congratulations, new converts and you who have decided to rededicate your life to Christ! God has chosen you to be the builders in His Kingdom. **"Jesus saith unto them, Did ye never read in the scriptures, the stone which the builders rejected, the same has become the head of the corner: this is the Lord's doing, and it is marvelous in our eyes? Therefore say I unto you, The Kingdom of God shall be taken from you, and given to a nation bringing forth the fruits thereof. And whosoever shall fall on this stone shall be broken: but on whomsoever it shall fall, it will grind him to powder'" (Matthew 21:42-44)**. In this passage of scripture, Jesus is in the temple (the house of God) teaching the chief priests (the pastors), the elders (the ministers), and the Jewish people (the congregation). Please see **Matthew 21:23.** Notice how Jesus reminded them of what they had read in God's Word. The builders are men and women who possess the Kingdom of God, but have built it with their own ideas, wisdom and desires. Jesus informed them that there is a stone that they'd rejected while they were in the process of building.

Then, He told them that God has made that same stone to become the head of the corner. Accept it or reject it. This is the Lord's doing, and it is marvelous in our eyes.

These people may or may not have known it was Jesus who they were rejecting, but today, we know that there is only one name whereby men will be saved—and that name is "Jesus" **(Acts 4:10-12)**. Notice in **verse 11** that the Apostle Peter also reminds the Jews of the stone which they'd rejected. Again, it is important that you understand that while they rejected the stone, God still made Him the head. Remember, God said, "**My people are destroyed for the lack of knowledge: because thou has rejected knowledge, I will also reject thee, that thou shalt be no priest to me: seeing thou hast forgotten the law of thy God, I will also forget thy children" (Hosea 4:6).**

As a new convert, you need to see how God wants to use you to win souls for His Kingdom, not in "the sweet by and by", but through sweat and demonstration right here and now.

Let's go back to **Matthew 21:43.** Notice that Jesus is the speaker and He informs the people who'd rejected Him that the Kingdom of God will be taken from them. Now, this is where you come in, my born- again brothers and sisters. The Kingdom shall be given to a nation bringing forth the fruits thereof, which means you have to produce fruit for the Kingdom of God. Also, please take notice of the fact that Jesus says the Kingdom will be taken from them, which means they must have possessed it, but due to the lack of production, it was repossessed. Now, you may ask, "How can I produce fruit when I don't even have any scriptures memorized yet?" Well, just remember, it's not what you know that makes the difference, it's who you know. In fact, it's more about who knows you. Remember when Jesus spoke of some people confessing about their faithful service to Him? Look at **Matthew 7:22; it reads, "Many will say to Me in that day, Lord, Lord, have we not prophesied in thy name? and in thy name have cast out devils? And in thy name done many wonderful works?"** Jesus never disputed whether they had done these things or not. Just listen to His direct response in **verse 23. "And then will I profess unto them, I never knew you: depart from Me, ye that work iniquity."** What He is saying is that many think they know me and are doing what I want when, truthfully, I don't know them and don't want them around Me because they've been doing what they want. The word iniquity means wickedness. Like I said, it's about who knows you. As Christ gets to know you, the more you begin to look like Him.

In **Matthew 21:16**, Jesus proclaims, **"Out of the mouth of babes and sucklings thou hast perfected praise."** This scripture is saying that even though you are babes in the Kingdom, you have been endowed with a garment of praise that has been perfected by the Holy Spirit who abides in you. You may ask, "What is the garment of praise that the Holy Spirit has perfected?" It's the same testimony that all members of the body of Christ possess— "I once was lost, but now I'm found, was blind, but now I see." When you add this to the rest of your testimony, and someone asks you, "Who found you?" you simply respond with "Jesus!" Now, you know you were lost, and you know that you were blind, but knowing that didn't change your situation. It was when you accepted Jesus Christ as your personal Lord and Savior that you were changed. It is through your relationship with Him that things begin to change in your life. Repentance will be manifested.

In **Galatians 5:7-9**, Paul asked the believers of the Church at Galatia a question that has echoed for more than two thousand years. This church had once functioned well, but all of a sudden, they had fallen into sin. Apostle Paul asked them who had hindered them that they would not obey the truth. He confirmed that this hindrance was not from God. Immediately thereafter, he stated, **"A little leaven leaveneth the whole lump."** The word "leaven" represents corruption, unsound doctrine, and hindrance to obey God's truth. Still today, there is leaven in the church, but God is going to remove it. In **Matthew 21:43**,

Jesus proclaimed that the Kingdom of God shall be given to a nation bringing forth the first-fruits of the Kingdom. **"But ye are a chosen generation, a royal priesthood, a holy nation, a peculiar people; that ye should show forth the praises of Him who hath called you out of darkness into His marvelous light" (1 Peter 2:9)**. This means that God has chosen you to be priests within a holy nation of peculiar people —a nation that produces more peculiar people.

Finally, **"As newborn babes, desire the sincere milk of the Word, that ye may grow thereby (1 Peter 2:2).** Now, drink all of your milk because it's time for "show and tell". Decide that you are going to show and tell someone everyday what the Lord has done in your life. Thus, your ministry begins, and the fruit of the Kingdom will come forth. Hallelujah! Say, "I DO" and do what He tells you to do!

Chapter 7

Different Strokes for Different Folks

Have you ever heard the expression, "Different strokes for different folks?" This statement carries more truth than a lot of people care to acknowledge. The truth of the matter is that God intended for us to be individuals with different personalities. He also gave all of us the choice to become one with Him by his Holy Spirit and through His Son. This means that there are diversities of people in the church, which explains the diversities of missions for the church, which justifies the necessity for diversities of Pastors of the church. Paul told the Church of Corinth, **"There are diversities of gifts, but the same Spirit. And there are differences of administrations, but the same Lord. And there are diversities of operations, but it is the same God which worketh all in all"** (1 Corinthians 12:4-6).

To get the full impact of this lesson, we must retreat to the book of beginnings **(Genesis 1:26-27)** to see how the Creator created His creation. This passage of scripture tells us that God created man in His own image, after His likeness. Notice that God says, **"Let us make**

man in our image, after our likeness." Here, He is referring to Himself in three persons: Father, Son and Holy Spirit, otherwise known as the Trinity. Likewise, man is a triune being. Man is a spirit who has a soul that lives in a body. So, we are all alike when it comes to creation, which means that we all have some of the Creator in us. The reason I am bringing this to your attention is because we need to understand and appreciate other people's uniqueness and freedom of choice so that when people do not act or react the way we think they should, we can respect their differences.

This must be dealt with in order for us to be available to minister where the Spirit leads and to whomever, regardless of what they look or act like. This is why Paul reminds us in **2 Corinthians 5:18-20, "And all things are of God, who hath reconciled us to himself by Jesus Christ, and hath given to us the ministry of reconciliation, to wit, that God was in Christ, reconciling the world unto himself, not imputing their trespasses unto them; and hath**

committed unto us the word of reconciliation. Now then we are ambassadors for Christ, as though God did beseech you by us; we pray you in the Christ's stead, be ye reconciled to God."

Now, in verse 18, brother Paul confirms what we've learned from Genesis, and that is that all things are of God. It doesn't matter how bad you feel a person is, how ugly you say a person is, how intelligent you think a person is, or even how poor you believe a person is. "All things" means all things, which includes Lottie, Dottie and every blessed body. So, what is the Apostle Paul saying in this passage of Scripture? Basically, we are all of God, but those of us who have received Jesus have been reconciled back to God. In turn, we have been given the ministry of reconciliation, meaning, our job is to reconcile others back to God. Just as God was in Christ working to bring the world back unto Himself, and not charging men's sins against them, He has also commissioned us to preach the message of reconciliation. Now, we are ambassadors for Christ; we are vessels that

God uses to appeal to unbelievers. So, just as Christ took our place on the cross, we should be reconciled to God and take Christ's place here in the world. Second Corinthians 5:19 says that God was in Christ, reconciling the world to Himself. So, He is in us reconciling the world to Himself by Jesus Christ. **"Little children, you are from God and have overcome them, for He who is in you is greater than he who is in the world" (1 John 4:4).**

Since we now understand our mission, let us take a look at the ultimate example of God's love in action, unselfishly embracing all kinds of people. Here, we have Jesus, who was conceived by the Holy Ghost. He was born of a teenage girl of Hebrew descent who had the blood of many nations in her veins. Jesus ministered first to His brethren (the Israelites), but rejoiced in the faith of a Syro-Phoenician woman and a Roman soldier. He ate dinner in the homes of Publicans and Pharisees. He even dined with sinners. He befriended a man who followed Him closely—a man who eventually chose to betray Him and sell Him out for thirty pieces of silver. He suffered His cross to be carried by an Ethiopian, and He embraced and forgave a confessed thief during His dying hours. Even after His death, burial and resurrection, Jesus appeared first to a woman who He had previously delivered from seven evil spirits and commissioned her to spread the good news. As the writer of **Hebrews 12:2-3** stated, **"Looking unto Jesus the author and finisher of our faith, who for the joy that was set before him endured the cross, despising the shame and is set down at the right hand of the throne of God. For consider him that endureth such contradiction of sinners against himself, lest ye be wearied and faint in your minds."** So, just keep looking to Jesus and be prepared to minister different strokes of God's love to different folks. With this, you will also learn to receive and appreciate the ministries of and from different folks who are led by God's Spirit. Shout Glory to God as you DIE in ObeDIEnce!

Chapter 8

Clothe Yourself With Love and Compassion

How do you clothe yourself with love and compassion? In **Colossians 3:12-15**, the Apostle Paul tell us to **"Put on therefore, as the elect of God, Holy and beloved, bowels of mercies, kindness, humbleness of mind, meekness, longsuffering; Forbearing one another, and forgiving one another, if any man have a quarrel against any; even as Christ forgave you, so also do ye. And above all these things put on Charity (love) which is the bond of perfectness. And let the peace of God rule in your hearts, to the which also ye are called in one body; and be thankful."**

Notice how we are told to put on bowels of mercies, kindness, humbleness of mind, meekness, longsuffering, and forbearance. These are all ingredients of compassion. Also mentioned was forgiveness, but His recipe of compassion demands that we wear the garment of love. This means you must show the love of God before you can show Godly compassion.

Did you know that even sinners can show compassion? It's true. Even the hardest, meanest criminal can show compassion, which is proof that everybody has a little bit of God in them. We are made in His image, after His likeness **(Genesis 1:26)**, but sin separates us from God. And the Bible tells us, **"Without shedding of blood is no remission" (Hebrews 9:22).** That is where Jesus comes in as the ultimate example of God's love. Christ is our only return flight back to God. He became the cross or the separation line between sinful and redeemed man. This is why **Matthew 26:27-28** states, **"And He took the cup and gave thanks, and gave it to them, saying, drink ye all of it; for this is My blood of the new testament, which is shed for many for the remission of sins."** Here, Jesus is speaking of a demonstration of faith in God. Notice how He says that the wine in the cup is His already shed blood. If you investigate this event, you will find that Jesus had not been to Calvary yet, nor had He shed any blood. It was His faith in God's Word that allowed Him to call things that were not as though they already were. It is our faith in God's love for us that will manifest as Godly compassion from us to others. The word "compassion" stirs up action. One definition for compassion is "eager yearning". It may be described as a particular expression of genuine love. It was compassion that became the driving force to cause Jesus to see so many circumstances develop against Him, and yet, continue on in love. Here is a heart-throbbing example of compassion towards all of mankind. In **Matthew 26:36-45**, Jesus went to Gethsemane with eleven of His disciples. Judas Iscariot was away, making arrangements to betray Jesus. Upon arriving at Gethsemane, Jesus instructed eight of his followers to sit there while He, Peter, and the two sons of Zebedee (James and John) went on to pray. He began to feel sorrowful and very heavy. He then instructed the three disciples to wait and watch with Him. In **Matthew 26:39**, Jesus falls on His face and prays these words: **"O My father, If it be possible, let this cup pass from me: nevertheless not as I will, but as thou wilt."** After praying, He went to the three disciples who were fast asleep and asked Peter,

"What, could ye not watch with me one hour? Watch and pray, that ye enter not into temptation: the spirit indeed is willing but the flesh is weak"(Matthew 26:40-41). He went away a second time and prayed, saying, **"O my Father, if this cup may not pass away from me, except I drink it, thy will be done" (Matthew 26:42).** And He came and found them asleep again for their eyes were heavy. And He left and went away again and prayed for the third time, saying the same words. Then He came to His disciples and said to them, **"Sleep on now, and take your rest: behold, the hour is at hand, and the Son of man is betrayed into the hands of sinners" (Matthew 26:45).**

During this hour of heaviness and sorrow, it is easy to see that our Lord was being bombarded with discouragement. Picture Him coming to the realization that the heaviness He was experiencing was dead weight in its truest form —the weight of the world (the dead) was coming down on His shoulders. Knowing that this was God's plan and His purpose, He still prayed and asked if the cup could pass from Him, but that petition came from His flesh. He immediately yielded to the Spirit and gave up His fleshly will. Keep in mind that He prayed the same prayer three times, and afterwards, He found the very ones He had counted on to watch and pray for Him in a helpless state of slumber. This made the situation look even more hopeless, because at one point, He scolded Peter for not successfully watching with Him for just an hour. Again, Jesus reminds Peter that the Spirit is indeed willing, but the flesh is weak. I believe that those words came from Jesus and also to Jesus. He encouraged Himself. Think about this— Is it possible that God allowed Jesus' brethren to become sleepy and useless in His time of need in order to verify that His prayer had been answered? "Yes, my Son, you must drink this cup—and you only!"

After three prayers to the Father, a shout for help at His friends, and a few fleshly moments, I believe it was compassion that brought Jesus to the attitude which was displayed in

Matthew 26:45. After Christ went through all that He had gone through, can you picture Him saying, "**If God said it, that settles it?**" I imagine He got up from the ground with a renewed spirit of joy, wiped Himself off and said, "I feel like going on!" Now, that is compassion. This compassion comes from love and leads to grace. Selah!

So, as you can see, love is the foundation, but without compassion, there is no salvation. And how do you know you are saved? John, the disciple whom Jesus loved, tells us, **"We know that we have passed from death unto life, because we love the brethren. He that loveth not his brother abideth in death" (1 John 3:14).** After this, the Apostle Paul instructs us to do good unto all men **(Galatians 6:10).** This is the change we should see once we are born again, which means we can no longer make the statement, "I have to love you, but I don't have to like you." If I don't like you, I can't love you unconditionally, but I can, however, not like what you do, yet still love you. Just remember to clothe yourself with love and compassion. And whenever you find it impossible, just listen to these words lovingly spoken by two of Jesus' followers, John and Peter: **"But whoso hath this world's good, and seeth his brother have need and shutteth up his bowels of compassion from him, how dwelleth the love of God in Him" (1 John 3:17)?** Finally, **"Be ye all of one mind, having compassion one of another, love as brethren, be pitiful, be courteous: not rendering evil for evil, or railing for railing, but contrariwise blessing; knowing that ye are thereunto called, that ye should inherit a blessing" (1 Peter 3:8-9).** I cannot possibly love like this unless I DIE in ObeDIEnce to CHRIST!

Chapter 9

Ex-Members of the Condemnation

"**There is therefore now no condemnation to them which are in Christ Jesus, who walk not after the flesh, but after the Spirit" (Romans 8:1).** There are varying nations existing in the world today. I am sure you have heard of the United Nations, Zulu Nation, Islamic Nation, Examination, Hallucination, and the Bible identifies Christians as a Holy Nation (**1 Peter 2:9)**. Mentioned here are just a few of the varying nations we are familiar with. But there is a nation mentioned in the Holy Bible that we should not be associated with, which is Condem-Nation.

We were all born as members of Condem-Nation, led by one destructive force called fear, and assisted by a stronghold called doubt. Fear and doubt are just two of the key players that make up the government of this nation—a nation that is ruled by Satan, the god of this world. In order to become members of the Holy Nation, we must be born again. We must be born into the Kingdom of God; this is made possible through Christ Jesus. Therefore, new converts must first be assured that they are new creations in Christ Jesus **(2 Corinthians 5:17)**. Even if we don't look, feel or talk new, we are made new by faith in God's Word. Remember, **we walk by faith and not by sight (2 Corinthians 5:7)**. So, when the Apostle Paul proclaims that there is no condemnation to them which are in Christ, he is saying that we cannot be in condemnation and also in Christ. There are ways to become associated with the Condem-Nation, and there are ways to avoid the Condem-Nation. Brothers and sisters, the answer is in your walk with Christ. The Word of God tells us how to walk and how not to walk as Christians. **Romans 8:13** explains that we should not walk after the flesh, but after the Spirit. After understanding this truth, we must walk in it. So, if we find ourselves being lured back into the Condem-Nation, we need to evaluate ourselves personally before crossing that boundary again. We do this by asking ourselves, "Am I walking in the flesh or in the Spirit?" Remember that God's Spirit will never lead us into condemnation, but our flesh will take us there in a heartbeat.

The Greek word for condemnation is "katakrima," which is defined as, "The sentence pronounced or the judgment with a suggestion of punishment following." We are all born in sin and shaped in iniquity, and the wages of sin is death. We are all guilty of sin, and by the law, all of us should be sentenced to death and hell. Thank God for Jesus! He paid the price that set us free from a destiny that was deservingly ours by becoming sin for us. **"For He hath made Him to be sin for us, who knew no sin; that we might be made the righteousness of God in Him" (2 Corinthians 5:21).**

This is where fear and doubt come into view. They are Satan's demonic assassins who destroy those who are without Christ. They also try to destroy those of us who are in Christ by attempting to steal God's Word from our hearts and minds. If we, God's people, allow fear and doubt to overtake our minds, we leave ourselves open to their mission—that mission is to cause God's people to commit spiritual suicide. In understanding that God has preserved us to be fruitful and to multiply His Kingdom, we must also understand that we cannot accomplish God's mission if we are overcome by fear and doubt. Fear and doubt are hindrances that work hand-in-hand. When we allow doubt (unbelief) to enter our minds, we can be assured that fear will follow. In the same way, when fear is present, doubt is present because fear causes doubt; they always work together. Fear seeks to destroy our faith in God, and doubt seeks to destroy our ability to perform our duties for God.

Romans 8:15 tells us, **"For ye have not received the spirit of bondage again to fear; but ye have received the Spirit of adoption, whereby we cry, Abba, Father."** Then, we are told in **2 Timothy 1:7, "For God has not given us the spirit of fear; but of power, and of love, and of a sound mind."** Isn't that just like God to give us three for one—we give up fear, and in return, He gives us power, love, and a sound mind? What an increase! In **Proverbs 12:2** we learn that **"A good man obtaineth favor of the Lord: but a man of wicked devices will he**

condemn." Did you know that there are eight groups of people who God has specifically condemned to spend eternity in Hell? In **Revelation 21:8**, Apostle John states, **"But the fearful, and unbelieving, and the abominable, and murderers, and whoremongers, and sorcerers, and idolaters, and all liars, shall have their part in the lake which burneth with fire and brimstone: which is the second death."** Most Christians are familiar with this verse, especially the six categories of people condemned by God. We tend to ignore the first two—the fearful and the unbelieving. The spirit of fear produces the "fearful" and doubt produces "unbelievers".

Here is a little food for thought. Compare **Revelation 21:8** with **Revelation 22:14-15**, where John proclaims, **"Blessed are they that do his commandments, that they may have right to the tree of life, and may enter in through the gates into the city. For without are dogs and sorcerers, and whoremongers, and murders, and idolaters, and whosoever loveth and maketh a lie."** Notice that both passages show the same groups listed; except in **Revelation 22:15**, the fearful, unbelieving, and abominable are not shown. Could it be possible that these three groups are categorized as "dogs?" That is another study worth conducting. At any rate, we should understand why those of us who are in Christ must remain ex-members of the Condem-Nation. If we do, we will know for sure that we have victory over fear and doubt.

Always remember that fear and doubt can condemn us, causing us to lose our desire to press towards the mark of the high calling. If we also believe and remember **1 John 4:18**, it will help us to conquer the enemy for **"There is no fear in love; but perfect love casteth out fear: because fear hath torment. He that feareth is not made perfect in love."** As Christians, we can rest in knowing that the Spirit of Love will convict us until we allow our wrongs to be corrected. He will lead us to sing a new song. So, say goodbye to the Condem-Nation, and say hello to the free and new creation that you have become. I DO!

Chapter 10

If You Don't Fall Down, You'll Never Get Up

Most of us are familiar with the television advertisement that features the famous statement **"I've fallen and I can't get up!"** Well, in the Kingdom of Heaven, you must fall on your knees in humility to be exalted in Christ Jesus **(1 Peter 5:6)**. So, since we must fall, let's all fall in love. I don't mean the way the world falls in love, which is usually a sexual or friendship kind of love that is based on what they will receive for what they have given. No! I'm talking about agape (unconditional) love that can only come from God, our Father, and through His Son, Jesus. Jesus is the ultimate example of God's unconditional love for all mankind **(John 3:16).**

There will be many times that we will miss God or fall short of where God wants us to be, but let us be encouraged, my brothers and sisters. Each time we fall or fail, we have to know that **"God is faithful and just to forgive us for our sins and to cleanse us from all unrighteousness; that is, if we confess our sins (1John 1:9)."** This is how we get up—by releasing that unnecessary weight and sin that holds us down, therefore, hindering us from growing to the level of fruitfulness that God has called us to manifest **(Hebrews 12:1)**.

Here is a personal testimony of how I grew up after taking a fall. The situation happened a few years ago at a time when I was a baby in Christ and feeling as if it was my responsibility to save the world. I was sincerely trying, but I was also sincerely wrong. In most cases, I just stirred up strife, rather than salvation. Basically, I was taught to look down on sinners, rather than get down with sinners and still not sin. So, then came the time when the Lord helped me to increase my faith. I had begun to see a manifestation of gifts, such as healing, the casting out of demons, prophesying and speaking in other tongues. If the Lord had not actually demonstrated these supernatural works through me, I'm not sure if I would have believed. I mean, I believed God could do anything, but I was taught that these signs were for the five-fold ministry. I was only what some Christians consider a "layman." Still, the more I made myself available, the more God used me. The more God used me, the more my faith grew, layman and all.

Then, here comes the fall. I was helping others to get their healing and deliverance by faith, and God was truly with me. A word was spoken to me, saying that I had been healed from diabetes. I was told to stop taking my insulin as a show of my faith, and then, I was to make an appointment with my doctor and tell him that God had healed me. Knowing that I had continuously exercised faith in God, I then asked myself, "Is my faith wavering? Why is everyone else getting healed through my faith while I remain sick?" Well, the doubt set in and that's when I realized that there is a thin line between faithfulness and foolishness.

I woke up the next morning, praising God for my healing and was determined to never again take insulin for diabetes. I went to work (I was a barber stylist who worked by appointment) and was feeling fine throughout the day. That was until about 3:30 that afternoon when faith vanished and the foolishness appeared. I began to feel dizzy, disoriented, nervous and confused. It was easy to recognize that God was with me, even in my failure. You see, I had just finished my last appointment on the books and my wife was already on standby, ready to come rescue me with insulin in hand. As a matter of fact, she had already called me twice to see how I was doing. So, after I called, she was there handing my insulin to me within about ten to twelve minutes. Sisters and brothers, that's discernment! Anyway, I injected my insulin and closed the barbershop. While my wife drove me home, I prayed to God, asking Him to forgive me for failing Him and for displaying such weak faith. Then, in a small but clear voice, the same Scripture I spoke of earlier **(1 John 1:9)** came to me again saying, **"God is faithful and just to forgive you of your sins and cleanse you from all unrighteousness."** But I had to take the first step. I had to confess my faults.

By the time I received that revelation, we had arrived home. I was still a little weak and wobbly, but I thank God that even in a weak and shaky state of mind, the Holy Spirit still ministered to me. The Holy Spirit ministered to me in a way that stirred up my faith—a faith that had raised me above the failure and the potentially deadly mistake I had made.

"Therefore being justified by faith, we have peace with God through our Lord Jesus Christ: By whom also we have access by faith into this grace wherein we stand, and rejoice in hope of the glory of God. And not only so, but we glory in tribulations also: knowing that tribulation worketh patience; And patience, experience, and experience, hope: And hope maketh not ashamed; because the love of God is shed abroad in our hearts by the Holy Ghost, which is given unto us. For when we were yet without strength, in due time Christ died for the ungodly" (Romans 5:1-6). In this passage of Scripture, Paul gives the prescription for a successful, fruitful life as servants in the Kingdom of God. Notice in the third verse, he says we are to glory in tribulations, knowing that tribulations work patience. Then, in the fourth verse, he speaks of patience working experience, and experience bringing hope.

To glory means "to shine or glow". The only way for us to shine during failures or hard times is to be assured that our patience is being cultivated through experience, and our experiences give us hope that no matter what comes next, we're going to make it. Now hear this—the world will tell you that experience is the best teacher, but through spiritual eyes, the Holy Spirit is the best teacher. Why? Because He teaches us to appreciate someone else's experience and to learn from it as if we have gone through it ourselves, minus the bumps and bruises, of course. In my case, even though I appeared to fail the test because I took my medication, I still passed the recovery test, which is where humility comes in. You see, as soon as I confessed my mess to my wife, and later to another brother who called to see how I was doing, the Lord immediately allowed me to go to sleep and rest. When I awakened the next morning, I felt brand new as if there had never been a problem. Look at

God! I didn't miss a day of work, I didn't see or even talk to a doctor (except Dr. Jesus), and I didn't take any medication, outside of my normal prescription.

I'm telling you, we are going to fall, but we can no longer say, "I can't get up." In **Philippians 4:13**, Paul says, **"I can do all things through Christ which strengtheneth me."** In closing, let me show how Christ strengthens me. **1 John 12:32**, Jesus warned the world and Satan about the effects of lifting Him up. He said, **"And I, if I be lifted up from the earth, will draw all men unto me." When Jesus was nailed to the cross, everyone had counted Him as "down and out"**. Can you just picture ole Satan and his imps celebrating, or picture Jesus' followers, who had great expectations, crying in a useless state of helplessness, because of what appeared to be a failure? Apparently, they all must have forgotten or they just did not believe God's Word, but again, I say that God is faithful. He didn't forget Jesus, and He won't forget you. Even if everyone else forgets you, God said, **"I will never leave thee or forsake** thee" **(Hebrews 13:5)**. I believe that Jesus remained obedient in order to be lifted up on Calvary's cross, because He knew who He was and is. In **Matthew 27:42-43**, some of the Jews mocked Him saying, **"He saved others; himself he cannot save. If he be the King of Israel, let him now come down from the cross, and we will believe him. He trusted in God; let him deliver him now, if he will have him; for he said, I am the Son of God."** Do you know who you are? Do you know whose you are? Remember when all else fails, God never fails! There is a one letter difference in the spelling of the word f-a-l-l and f-a-i-l. The letter i. This reminds me that I am the difference between whether I fall or fail. To fail, many times, alludes to an ending or termination, but to fall reminds me that I can get back up and try again. He will pick you up, turn you around and place your feet on solid ground. Hallelujah! I Die in ObeDIEnce!

Chapter 11

Set Up from the Neck Up

Many times, in a life filled with ups and downs, we are constantly taking low blows from people who lack Godly compassion, and Satan always aims for our heads. He tries to convince us that we are "tore up from the floor up." But I have good news for you. We've been "set up from the neck up." The believer's authority comes from the head. Let me explain.

When I speak of authority, I'm referring to power or dominion. All authority comes from God. **"But I would have you know, that the head of every man is Christ; and the head of the woman is the man; and the head of Christ is God" (1 Corinthians 11:3).** All authority comes from the head. **Matthew 28:18** says, **"And Jesus came and spake unto them, saying, All power is given unto me in heaven and in earth."** All authority comes from the head. **"Go ye therefore, and teach all nations, baptizing them in the name of the Father, and the Son, and the Holy Ghost: Teaching them to observe all things whatsoever I have commanded you: an lo, I am with you always, even unto the end of the world. Amen (Matthew 28:19-20).** All authority comes from the head. **"And he gave some, apostles and some, prophets; and some, evangelists; and some, pastors and teachers (Ephesians 4:11).** All authority comes from the head. **"But as many as received him, to them gave he power to become the sons of God, even to them that believe on his name (John 1:12).** Again, I say, all authority comes from the head. When this truth is acknowledged, it becomes easier to submit to authority. We become less likely to try to take authority and more likely to try to receive authority that is given to us. Jesus said, **"But ye shall receive power, after that the Holy Ghost is come upon you: and ye shall be witnesses unto me..." (Acts 1:8).** Any authority given to believers must come from God, the head of Christ, and through Jesus Christ, the head of the church, and through the Holy Spirit who bears witness with our spirit. The above examples of authority all begin with the head, and there are many more expressed throughout the scriptures. Satan is also familiar with the fact that authority comes from the head. This is why he constantly attacks your physical head (mouth, tongue, eyes, ears and mind). I mean, we are talking about a character who actually tried to take authority from The Authority! Lucifer was an anointed, beautiful angel before he fell from Heaven and became Satan. The prophet, Isaiah, gives this account of the fall: **"How art thou fallen from heaven, O Lucifer, son of the morning! How art thou cast down to the ground, which didst weaken the nations! For thou hast said in thine heart, I will ascend into heaven, I will exalt my throne above the stars of God. I will sit also upon the mount of the congregation, in the sides of the north: I will ascend above the heights of the clouds; I will be like the most High" (Isaiah 14:12:14).** Here, we can see how Lucifer tried to lift his (God-given) authority above his Authority (God). The problem with the words that were spoken here was not so much Lucifer's desire to be closer to God, or to be above the clouds and the stars of God, or even to be like the Most High God, because even believers are expected to live Godly by being transformed into the image of Christ. No, that wasn't the problem. Just look how many times

Lucifer said, "I" in just one sentence. He said it five times! I will delve deeper into Lucifer's "I" problem in Chapter 16. Now God had given him authority, but suddenly, he desired to take God's authority. So, it is plainly shown that he goes for the head, understanding that all authority comes from the head.

Now, why does he attack our heads? First of all, it seems that too many believers misunderstand how God's Word explains that all authority comes from the head. You see, we have reversed this authority issue. I mean the devil is not supposed to beat us upside our heads; we're supposed to be dancing on his head. In the Garden of Eden, the Lord God said to Satan, the serpent, **"I will put enmity between thee and the woman, and between thy seed and her seed; it shall bruise thy head, and thou shalt bruise his heel" (Genesis 3:15).** So, if we have bruises, they should be on our feet, not on our heads. This is why I say, "we've been set up from the neck up." God set us up good and proper. He has given us authority as believers, but this authority is found in our heads. Just look at the power that God has invested in our heads—an authority that authorizes us to live victorious lives.

First, we have a mouth to speak the Word and confess the Lord Jesus as Savior. **Romans 10:9** says, **"That if thou shalt confess with thy mouth the Lord Jesus, and shalt believe in thine heart that God hath raised him from the dead, thou shalt be saved."** Second, in our mouths, we have a tongue that can either whip Satan or work for Satan. I believe that positive speech leads to a positive life, and spiritual talk leads to a spiritual walk. **"Death and life are in the power of the tongue: and they that love it shall eat the fruit thereof" (Proverbs 18:21).** Third, we have eyes to see the natural, but believers have spiritual eyes that can see the supernatural. They are eyes of faith. **"For we walk by faith, not by sight" (1 Corinthians 5:7).** Forth, we have ears to hear what the Lord is saying with divine clarity. **"So, then faith cometh by hearing, and hearing by the Word of God" (Romans 10:17).** Last but not least, we have a renewed mind. **"And be not conformed**

to this world: but be ye transformed by the renewing of your mind, that ye may prove what is that good, and acceptable, and perfect, will of God" (Romans 12:2). God's Word says, **"Let this mind be in you, which was also in Christ Jesus" (Philippians 2:5).**

Remember, all of these weapons of authority are gifts from the Head of authority, and just like every other gift, God will never force us to use them. We can be like the first Adam (in the Garden of Eden) and let the devil take our minds, or we can be like the last Adam (in the Garden of Gethsemane) and make the devil mind us! We praise you, Jesus! I DO! Now, what about you?

Chapter 12

Followin' Christ or in Christ?

I'm learning that many believers become Christians then lose their identity by becoming complacent. I believe we all start our Christian walks by following Christ, but as we continue on our journey, we must mature in Christ. We can compare following Jesus to making Him the Savior of our lives; we can compare being in Jesus to making Him Lord of our lives. In order for us to know our identities in Him, we must first know His identity in us. **"And He said to them all, if any man will come after me, let him deny himself, and take up his cross daily, and follow me. For whosoever will save his life shall lose it; but whosoever will lose his life for my sake, the same shall save it" (Luke 9:23-24).** Here, Jesus is saying if you follow Him, there are some prerequisites involved. Deny thyself and take up your cross. After this, you can follow Him. In the natural, denying yourself would mean losing your identity, but in the realm of the spirit, it's actually just the opposite. Jesus says, if you lose your life (your identity) for His sake, you shall save it. There are many distractions that cause us to forget who we are as we attempt to follow Jesus. We actually lose focus on Him. That's why the Apostle Paul said, **"Casting down imaginations, and every high thing that exalteth itself against the knowledge of God, and bringing into captivity every thought to the obedience of Christ" (2 Corinthians 10:5).** If we don't continue to focus on Jesus, the cares of this world will eventually draw our attention away from our leader. We have to walk in the Spirit, so we won't satisfy the lusts of the flesh **(Galatians 5:16).** This is what Jesus was saying in reference to denying yourself. **"And they that are Christ's have crucified the flesh with the affections and lusts. If we live in the spirit, let us also walk in the Spirit" (Galatians 5:24-25).** When Jesus was ready to ascend to Heaven, He told His disciples that He had prayed for the Father to send another Comforter (the Spirit of Truth). In **John 14:25-26,** He explains, **"These things have I spoken unto you, being present with you. But the Comforter, which is the Holy Ghost, whom the Father will send in My name, He shall teach you all things, and bring all things to your remembrance, whatsoever I have said unto**

you." Here, Jesus is showing us the only way to follow Him. We must be led by the Spirit, who will teach us and bring all things to our remembrance that Jesus has told us. By the way, this is the same Spirit that led Jesus during His earthly ministry, even into the wilderness when He was tempted by the devil **(Luke 4:1-2).**

The only way we can be in Christ is to become new creatures **(2 Corinthians 5:17).** We become new creatures with the assistance of the Holy Spirit. He guides us into all truth. This is why when Jesus was with His disciples in the flesh, He told them to follow Him. He knew that when His appointed time came that their appointed time would come also, and they would need power to walk in the newness of life in Him **(Acts 1:8).** Knowing our identity in Christ is the key to a victorious life in the midst of trials and tribulations. Identity or identification (I.D.) is what identifies who we are and to whom we belong. So, I submit to you my brothers and sisters that the I.D. of a seasoned believer is in Christ, not following

Christ. The only way to successfully follow Christ is to get into Him and allow Him to get into you. In **Matthew 11:28-30,** Jesus said, **"Come unto me, all ye that labour and are heavy laden, and I will give you rest. Take my yoke upon you and learn of me; for I am meek and lowly in heart; and ye shall find rest into your souls. For my yoke is easy, and my burden is light."** If you are tired and worn down from trying to follow Jesus, don't be discouraged. He promised to give us rest. Just get connected in becoming one with Jesus, and you will find rest for your soul. I would like to close this chapter with the lyrics from a song that should be the testimony of all who are in Christ. The name of this hymn is *In the Garden*, by C. Austin Miles. As these words enter your spirit and you make them personal, it won't matter what goes on around you or what the devil tries to do, you can know that your identity remains in Jesus Christ. What a fellowship!

I come to the garden alone
While the dew is still on the roses

And the voice I hear, falling on my ear
The Son of God discloses
He speaks, and the sound of His voice
Is so sweet the birds hush their singing
And the melody that He gave to me
Within my heart is ringing
I'd stay in the garden with Him
Tho' the night around me be falling
But He bids me go; through the voice of woe
His voice to me is calling
And He walks with me, and He talks with me
And He tells me I am His own;
And the joy we share as we tarry there
None other has ever known.

The joy of the Lord is my strength. My strength
is the joy of the Lord! That's my identity in Him.
I Die in ObeDIEnce to live in Him.

Chapter 13

Pray to Fast

Prayer and fasting are two powerful weapons that new converts need to put into effect immediately to be victorious in the growth process that God is bringing us through. Prayer is more than falling on your knees, bowing your head, folding your hands and closing your eyes, and then bombarding God with flattering words to pump Him up in preparation for your subtle presentation of a wish list. No, Beloved! That is not prayer. It is a fraudulent get-over mentality that has been birthed of the devil and administered to and through the church. Many of us have actually been taught this method of prayer! Our lives should be full of prayer, but prayer is ineffective without meditation. This is true because prayer is communion with God, not to God. Prayer is a two-way communication, where God speaks and we listen, and we speak and God listens. Most of us know how to speak to God, but are struggling with how to listen to God. In other words, we know how to say, "Lord I want" or "Lord, can I have?" We know how to say, "Lord give us this day." But Webster's Dictionary defines the word "meditate" as "to plan or intend: to think deeply." So, what should we meditate on? In **Philippians 4:8,** the Apostle Paul gives us a list of things to meditate on: **"Finally, brethren, whatsoever things are true, whatsoever things are honest, whatsoever things are just, whatsoever things are pure, whatsoever things are lovely, whatsoever things are of good report; if there be any virtue, and if there be any praise, think on these things."** He mentions thinking on things that are true, honest, just, pure, lovely, of good report, virtuous and praise worthy. The scripture is not a problem, nor are the things in the scripture, but the problem is the fact that many of us don't know God's definition of these things. In other words, we don't know what God considers to be true, honest, just, pure, lovely, of good report, virtuous, and praise worthy. This can only be discovered through knowing Him personally. The way we get to know Him is by studying His Word. This is revealed through the Son of God and the will of God. It is revealed through His Logos (the Word), which is contained within the pages of the Holy Bible from Genesis to Revelation. As we learn of Him through His Word, we recognize the written or spoken (Rhema) Word, which is a Word that is especially formulated for us directly from God. Upon understanding this, we understand the importance of having meditation incorporated in prayer, because when we pray, there should be a desire to hear from God. If we don't know the person and the character of God through knowing the Word of God, we may be deceived into thinking that we've heard from Him when, in actuality, we have not! **And no marvel, for Satan himself is transformed into an angel of light" (2 Corinthians 11:14).** We cannot imagine who or what God is because He's so much greater than our imaginations. **"Greater is he that is in you, than he that is in the world" (1 John 4:4). "Casting down imaginations, and every high thing that exalteth itself against the knowledge of God, and bringing into captivity every thought to the obedience of Christ" (2 Corinthians 10:5).** We must know Him to discern His voice from the many deceptive voices of the enemy, the flesh, the world, and the devil. In the book of

Hebrews, the writer gives us an invitation to pray with authority. He says, **"Let us therefore come boldly unto the throne of grace, that we may obtain mercy, and find grace to help in time of need" (Hebrews 4:16).** So, when we come into God's presence through prayer, we are confident that He will be merciful to us and give us grace to help when we are in need. That is why Paul firmly states , **"But my God shall supply all your needs according to His riches in Glory by Jesus Christ" (Philippians 4:19).** With this in mind, we can stop praying for "things" and learn to accept the grace which was given through the blood Jesus shed on Calvary's cross. **"And he said unto me, my grace is sufficient for thee. For my strength is made perfect in weakness" (2 Corinthians 12:9).**

Fasting is effective because we feed our spiritual man through prayer and meditation with God. Turning away meals or turning down our plates will make our bodies weak, but at the same time, it lifts our spirits. If you haven't heard God's voice concerning fasting, you are heading into a self-inflicted famine. Many victories have been won through prayer and fasting. In **Mark 9:29,** Jesus told his disciples, **"This kind can come forth by nothing but prayer and fasting."** King Darius fasted while Daniel was in the lion's den **(Daniel 6:18)**. The leaders of the Church at Antioch fasted and prayed as the Lord instructed them to separate Barnabas and Paul to go forth in ministry **(Acts 13:2-3)**. Today, husbands and wives are still encouraged to deprive each other only (upon mutual agreement) and give themselves to fasting and prayer **(1 Corinthians 7:5).**

At this time, I want to direct your attention to a passage of scripture that confirms the fact that fasting without prayer is deadly. It is very important that we remember prayer is communicating with God. (He talks to us and we listen; we talk to Him and He listens.) Listening is a large portion of the meditation process of prayer, but it must be followed up with application. To hear the fullness of what God is saying, we need to read **I Kings 13:1-33**. But for the purpose of saving time, here's a brief summary of this passage. There came a man of God out of Judah who was guided by the Lord into Bethel. He was to deliver the Word of the Lord. The man of God prayed and obeyed the instructions of the Lord, and God's Word came to pass. He even prayed to the Lord for Him to heal the king, and God answered. So, the king invited the man of God to come home with him for a reward, but the man of God refused the offer, because God had instructed him to fast. Let's read his testimony, **"For so was it charged me by the word of the Lord, saying, eat no bread, nor drink water, nor turn again by the same way that thou came to Bethel" (I Kings 13:9).** Again, he obeyed God, continued to fast and went another way. There was an old prophet that lived in Bethel whose sons told him what the Lord had done through the man of God. So, the old prophet went and found the man of God and invited him back with him to eat and drink. Again, he refused, reminding him of God's command. Now, look at **verse 18,** and you'll see where the man of God lost focus and communication with God. **"He said unto him, I am a prophet also as thou art; and an angel** spake unto me by the word of the Lord, saying, Bring him back with thee into thine house, that he may eat and drink water. But he lied unto him. So he went back with him, and did eat bread in his house, and drank water. And it came to pass, as they sat at the table, that the word of the Lord came unto the prophet that brought him back; and he cried unto the man of God that came from Judah, saying, Thus saith the Lord, For as much as thou has disobeyed the mouth of the Lord and has not kept the commandment which the Lord thy God commanded thee. But camest back, and hast eaten bread and drunk water in the place, of which the Lord did say to thee, eat no bread, and drink no water; thy carcass shall not come unto the sepulcher of thy fathers" (1 Kings 13:18-22).

There are so many lessons to be learned in this passage, but please take notice of how the man of God was obedient because of his communication and meditation with God, and how he failed to continue to fast because he'd listened to another man of God or should I say a "lying prophet", even after knowing what God had already told him. I know you're probably asking how was he supposed to know that a seasoned man of God whom he wanted to give the utmost respect to would attempt to lead him away from God? That's a good question and here are two fundamental Kingdom principles to guide you through situations like this.

Principle #1— **2 Corinthians 13:1, "In the mouth of two or three witnesses shall every word be established".**
Principle #2— **1 Thessalonians 5:12-13, "And we beseech you, brethren, to know them which labour among you, and are over you in the Lord, and admonish you; And to esteem them very highly in love for their work's sake. And be at peace among yourselves."**

If you do your research, you will discover that applying these two principles would have saved that young prophet's life. You can't allow just any and everybody to speak into your life, regardless of what their title might be. You must continue to get to know God, yet remember you're not the only one who knows Him. As you read on, you will find that the man of God was killed by a lion, but not devoured. I wonder why and why not? Beloved, we are also men and women of God and must always remember to pray and fast in order to continue to Die in ObeDIEnce to Christ!

Chapter 14

To Live is Christ

As Christians, it's time we realized that we are going to face trials, tribulations, sickness, hardships, hard times and even bad times. **1 Peter 4:12** says, **"Beloved, think it not strange concerning the fiery trial which is to try you, as though some strange thing happened unto you."** But, did you notice that the unsaved also go through trials? The problem with this situation is that there should be a difference between the way believers deal with trials versus the way unbelievers deal with them. The difference is that we are to endure the trials, not to try to pray them away or run away from them ourselves. The world is known for using methods of what I call escapism; for instance, drugs, alcohol, overeating, overworking, and sinful love affairs, which are all temporary fixes expected to help people escape trials.

The best way to endure trials is to understand the purpose of the trials. To endure means "to bear or stand firm." But, before we deal with endurance, we need to take a good look at the One who can prepare us to successfully endure the trials. The Apostle Paul looks at the Creator as a potter and us, the creation, as the clay. As we analyze this subject, please remain open to the Spirit of God because the revelation you're about to receive has absolutely destroyed man's theology of who God is and what He will or will not do. (Yet, we still try to put God in a box!) Let's begin with **Romans 9:20-24** (from the New Revised Standard Version). It reads, **"But who indeed are you, a human being to argue with God? Will what is molded say to the one who molded it, 'Why have you made me like this?' Has the potter no right over the clay, to make out of the same lump one object for special use and another for ordinary use? What if God, desiring to show his wrath and to make known his power, has endured with much patience the objects of wrath that are made for destruction; and what if he has done so in order to make known the riches of his glory for the objects of mercy, which he has prepared before-hand for glory-including us whom he has called, not from the Jews only, but also from the Gentiles?"** Basically, Paul is simply reminding us that the Potter is sovereign and can do what He wants to do with the clay. And if the lump of the clay is not molded or formed for the use that the Potter intended it, it is therefore the Potter's prerogative to re-form or reshape it as He sees fit. Now, after looking at God in the light of this passage of Scripture, we should find it senseless to murmur and complain about anything that God has done, is doing or even allows to be done in our lives.

To get a closer view of God's perspective of how He handles His creation, let's join the prophet Jeremiah and visit the potter's house. **"The word which came to Jeremiah from the LORD, saying, Arise, and go down to the potter's house, and there I will cause thee to hear my words. Then I went down to the potter's house, and behold, he wrought a work on the wheels. And the vessel that he made of clay was marred in the hand of the potter; so he made it again another vessel, as it seemed good to the potter to make it. Then the word of the Lord came to me saying, O house of Israel, cannot I do with you as this potter? saith the Lord. Behold, as the clay is in**

the potter's hand, so are ye in mine, O house of Israel" (Jeremiah 18:1-6). As you can see, there is extensive remodeling taking place at the potter's house. As He molds His creation in His hands, He realizes that it is not taking form as He designed it to be, so He places it back on the wheels and begins to mold and shape His production according to His specifications. Remember, Jesus is coming back for a church without spot or wrinkle, and this is how He gets the "spots and wrinkles" out!

Now, you may be wondering, "What does all this have to do with enduring trials and tribulations?" I believe that the Lord uses trials and tribulations to make us into the vessels He desires us to be. These trials represent tests, and we must keep in mind that a "test" is always the beginning of a "testimony." But, we must also remember that sometimes, because of disobedience, we can bring on trials that God never intended for us to go through. In other words, we get off the wheel and pick up more lumps and bumps; then, after we repent, we get back on the wheel and begin where we left off. We eventually come back to the same position, but we're in a worse condition! Now, God has to smooth out the bumps that He was originally working on, plus, He must smooth out new bumps! This can definitely backup the process, which brings a new meaning to the term backsliding. (See **1 Peter 4:15).** I DO ObeDIEnce to Christ!

Chapter 15

The Super 8 R's

Since we now understand that new converts and mature Christians alike must face trials, allow me to share the **eight R's** on how to endure trials. They are based on **1 Peter 5:6-11**.

1. **Reach** up to God and stay humble. **"Humble yourselves therefore under the mighty hand of God, that he may exalt you in due time" (1 Peter 5:6).**

2. **Release** your cares to God. **"Casting all your care upon him; for he careth for you" (1 Peter 5:7)**.

3. **Remain** disciplined and focused on God. **"Be sober and vigilant" (1 Peter 5:8)**.

4. **Realize** that Satan is already a defeated foe with a big mouth and no teeth. **"Because your adversary the devil, as a roaring lion walketh about, seeking whom he may devour" (1 Peter 5:8).**

5. **"Resist him steadfast in the faith, understanding that your brothers and sisters are also being tried" (1 Peter 5:9).**

6. **Rest** in knowing that you are called by God unto His eternal glory. **"But the God of all grace, who hath called us unto his**

eternal glory by Christ Jesus." (1 Peter 5:10).

7. **Remember** God's promises of renewal, restoration and rejuvenation after we pass the trial. **"... after that ye have suffered a while, make you perfect, stablish, strengthen, settle you"** (1 Peter 5:10).

8. **Rejoice** and give God glory always. **"To him be glory and dominion forever and ever. Amen"** (1 Peter 5:11).

Study these eight R's, especially before and after your trials. (During the trial, there are so many distractions that it's sometimes hard even to know what you should already know!) If we prepare ourselves and put on the whole armor of God, we will have much joy as we suffer with Christ. **"But rejoice, inasmuch as ye are partakers of Christ's sufferings; that is, when his glory shall be revealed, ye may be glad also with exceeding joy"** (1 Peter 4:13). As believers, we must accept the fact that to live is Christ, and Christ represents victory through suffering. **"Yet if any man suffer as a**

Christian, let him not be ashamed: but let him glorify God on this behalf" (I Peter 4:16). Now, let's join together and testify in submission to the Potter before our flesh, the world, and the devil by singing this famous chorus from *My Life Is In Your Hands*, written by the gifted and talented Kirk Franklin:

> I know that I can make it; I know that I can stand.
> No matter what may come my way,
> My life is in your hands.
> With Jesus, I can take it;
> With Him, I know I can stand.
> No matter what may come my way,
> My life is in Your hands.

If we understand and speak these words from our hearts, we can boldly say, **"For me to live is Christ, and to die is gain" (Philippians 1:21).** Now that we're in Christ, what more can we gain, especially if we should die? He is our all-in-all. So, when we die and go to Heaven, we'll have the same Christ that we had when we lived on Earth. But look at God's mathematics: our gain is actually a minus. As we live in Christ, we must suffer, and as we die in Christ, we suffer no more. Hallelujah! To die is gain. I DO! I Die in ObeDIEnce to Christ!

Chapter 16

Try the Spirits

"Beloved, believe not every spirit, but try the spirits whether they are of God: because many false prophets are going out into the world" (1 John 4:1).

Have you ever heard someone say, "Try the spirit by the spirit?" This statement sounds like an interpretation of what the Apostle John is saying in the above scripture, but that's not the full message implied here. I'll tell you how I know this to be true. You see, I've always wondered how a human being can take the life of another human being as if there was nothing to it. And I was trained by the U.S. Army to kill on command, yet even as a thirteen-year veteran, it still wasn't easy for me. This really hit home after the brutal murders of my grandson's father and cousin, who were both shot in the head. I'm saying this because this young man called me "Dad", and after his murder, I felt as if I had a gaping hole in my heart. So, I called my "Dad", which art in heaven, and He filled that hole until it began to overflow with revelation. **"Jesus stood and cried, saying, If any man thirst, let him come**

unto me, and drink. He that believeth on me, as the scripture hath said, out of his belly shall flow rivers of living water" (John 7:37). So, I came to Him and began to drink, and as He promised, here comes the overflow!

Let's deal with these spirits that Brother John is referring to in **1 John 4:1**. He tells us not to believe every spirit, which means that there are many spirits. Of course, there is the Holy Spirit, who is the one sent by God, and there are evil spirits, who have been sent by the devil. Spirits work by influence, but we can choose what we allow ourselves to be influenced by. This ability to choose is God-given, and everyone must act on it. Even babies have to choose what spirits they submit to; the problem is they don't know the difference between good and evil. They must be taught by example, not experience. This is why it's dangerous to teach someone to try the spirits by the spirits, because we must be sure our spirits are influenced by the Holy Spirit to test every other spirit.

With this understanding, let's examine one of the most damaging evil spirits working against the Kingdom of God: the spirit of pride. If there is any confusion as to which category the spirit of pride falls under, we need to go to **Isaiah 14:12-14.** Please remember that the focus of pride is self. Self says, "I've got to have it my way." Here, we have Lucifer, the archangel of God, created with magnificent splendor, full of wisdom and perfect in beauty. One day, iniquity was found in him, and that iniquity was the origin of sin **(Read Ezekiel 28:11-19).** If iniquity was found in him after God made him perfect, then Lucifer is the founder of sin. **"How art thou fallen from heaven, O Lucifer, son of the morning! how art thou cut down to the ground, which didst weaken the nations! For thou hast said in thine heart, I will ascend into heaven, I will exalt my throne above the stars of God: I will sit also upon the mount of the congregation, in the sides of the north: I will ascend above the heights of the clouds; I will be like the most high. Yet thou shalt be brought down to hell, to the sides of the pit"** (Isaiah 14:12-15). Can you see the spirit of pride manifesting itself throughout Lucifer's proclamation? The word that we want to focus on here is "I", which just so happens to be in the middle of sin (s -I-n). Wherever you find sin, there will always be an "I" initiating it. Please take notice that I is also in the middle of the word pride (p-r-I-d-e). Now **verse 15** confirms that the spirit of pride is not from God, because His reward to Lucifer for displaying this pride is a final destination to hell. So, we can now agree that the spirit of pride comes from the devil. If you drop the "d" in devil, you'll find the word "evil."

I know you may be wondering what pride has to do with cold-blooded murder? First, we need to clear up an incredible tale from the crypt concerning Black history. I'll start with a reminder that no one can curse what God has blessed. We've been taught that the Black race is an accursed people, and many lost souls have used the Bible to support this fable. And while many of us claim liberty by mouth, the seed is still planted in our minds that Noah's son, Ham, messed up and caused Black people to be accursed forever. Well, let's look at what God really has to say about this. Please read **Genesis 9:18-27.** It reads, **"And the sons of Noah, that went forth of the ark, were Shem, and Ham, and Japheth: and Ham is the father of Canaan. These are the three sons of Noah: and of them was the whole earth overspread. And Noah began to be an husbandman, and he planted a vineyard: And he drank of the wine, and was drunken; and he was uncovered within his tent. And Ham, the father of Canaan, saw the nakedness of his father, and told his two brethren without. And Shem and Japheth took a garment, and laid it upon both their shoulders, and went backward, and covered the nakedness of their father; and their faces were backward, and they saw not their father's nakedness. And Noah awoke from his wine, and knew what his younger son had done unto him. And he said, Cursed be Canaan; a servant of servants shall he be unto his brethren. And he said, Blessed be the Lord God of Shem; and Canaan shall be his servant. God shall enlarge**

Japheth, and he shall dwell in the tents of Shem; and Canaan shall be his servant."

A brief summary will show that Noah had three sons. One of them (Ham) looked upon his father's naked body, which was considered invasion of parental privacy. Now, Noah pronounced a curse as a result of this action, but for some reason, it was not on Ham. The curse came upon his son, Canaan. This has everything to do with **Genesis 9:1**, which shows God blessing Noah and his sons. In **verse 23,** we see Noah waking up from a drunken sleep and still having the presence of mind to know what had happened and who had been involved. **"And he said, cursed be Canaan; a servant of servants shall he be unto his brethren. And he said, blessed be the Lord God of Shem; and Canaan shall be his servant. God shall enlarge Japheth and he shall dwell in the tents of Shem; and Canaan shall be his servant" (Genesis 9:25-27).** Read it for yourself, get it in your spirit, and reverse the curse that never was at first. We are the descendants of Ham, and we are a blessed people, along with the white, red and yellow people. We're all a blessed people, but God gives us all the freedom to choose life or death as individuals.

"Behold, I set before you this day a blessing and a curse; a blessing if ye obey the commandments of the Lord your God, which I command you this day: And a curse, if ye will not obey the commandments of the Lord your God, but turn aside out of the way which I command you this day, to go after other Gods, which ye have not known" (Deuteronomy 11:26-28). The key to making the proper choice is based on which spirit we allow to influence our decisions. Under the influence of the spirit of pride, we have neither need nor desire to obey God's commandments because we have already established our own commandments. The spirit of pride caters to the flesh by means of a carnal mind. **"For to be carnally minded is death; but to be spiritually minded is life and peace. Because the carnal mind is enmity against God: for it is not subject to the law of God, neither indeed can be. So then they that**

are in the flesh cannot please God" (Romans 8:6-8). That's it! It's not a Black or White issue.

I remember some years back when we mourned the loss of the lives of four little girls and a teacher in Arkansas; they were all white. The alleged killers were two white guys, an eleven-year old and a thirty-year old. The devil is colorblind, except for when he sees the blood of Jesus. **"The thief cometh not, but for to steal and to kill, and to destroy: I am come that they might have life, and have it more abundantly" (John 10:10).** It's this same man, Jesus, who gave us the divine influence of the Holy Spirit to choose life and peace. Those who refuse to receive Him have instead, received the father of the spirit of pride (Satan). His influence leads to death. Paul says a spiritual mind is life and peace. This means you choose death and curses for others. You become a god in your mind, and from there, you react on your thoughts. If you do this, it makes you an enemy of God. This is what's happening to our young people of today, and this is why people are so quick to kill one another. Yes, they are responsible for their actions, but we, who are parents and believers, are responsible for their influences. It's not too late to make a change, but we've got to get real with God. Most of us know that if we go out into this war zone with carnal weapons, such as quoting scripture, pleading the blood of Jesus, speaking in tongues or even praying a prayer, the enemy is going to eat us alive. I said "carnal weapons", because if we are influenced by the spirit of pride to do any of these things, they then become carnal weapons. This is the reason we love to show off in the church building during Sunday service. It's usually the spirit of pride manifesting and expressing itself. Listen my brothers and sisters, we all love this scripture, but will we live it? **"Ye are of God, little children, and have overcome them: because greater is he that is in you, than he that is in the world" (1 John 4:4)**. Let's take Him to the streets so His influence will influence. Say, I DO to CHRIST!

Chapter 17

We Need 2-B-1

The title of this chapter could be considered confusing or even a false statement, and that's because, according to basic mathematics, the word "we" (meaning two or more) will never add up to one. Now, that's common sense! But, as believers, we need to begin with our spiritual senses, and then apply our common sense as the Spirit leads us. **"I beseech you therefore, brethren, by the mercies of God, that ye present your bodies a living sacrifice, holy, acceptable unto God, which is your reasonable service. And be not conformed to this world; but be ye transformed by the renewing of your mind; that ye may prove what is that good, and acceptable, and perfect will of God" (Romans 12:1-2).**

Throughout the entire Bible, God is continuously revealing the power of us becoming one. This can be witnessed from the book of Genesis to the Revelation of Jesus Christ, but all of these accounts of oneness were not God-ordained. Please notice how God intervenes and has the last word in each situation. As we travel together in confidence, that with the guidance of the Holy Spirit, we will know the difference between uniting "as one in common" versus "as one in Christ". To get the full benefits of this journey through the scriptures, you need to bring your Bible and a hearty appetite to receive a more enriched relationship with the Father.

First of all, we must agree that if we confess our belief in Him, we also profess that we have a relationship with Him (be it up close and personal or from a distance). The confession is in our talk, but the profession is in our walk. If we walk in harmony with the Lord, we'll share the same walk with one another and complete the circle of love, so that the world can witness and desire God's perfect love, which can only be found in Jesus Christ, the actual substance that holds it all together. He's a Keeper! Yes, He is!

So, let's take a look at some biblical examples of God's people who were on one accord and outside of the Lord's program. We'll begin in **Genesis 3:6. "And when the woman saw that**

**the tree was good for food, and that it was
pleasant to the eyes, and a tree to be desired
to make one wise, she took of the fruit
thereof, and did eat and gave also unto her
husband with her; and he did eat."** There is no
need to point fingers here. The man, woman,
and serpent were all on one accord and
without the Lord. In **Genesis 3:17**, God tells
Adam that since he agreed with his wife and
she agreed with the serpent, that the ground
was cursed because of their agreement. In
Genesis 3:19, he confirms His promise of sure
death. Remember, this is the result of agreeing
with one another and not with God. That's
enough power to short-circuit and fatally
condemn all humanity. Thank God for the
resurrection power of Jesus that redeems us
from that condemnation through eternity.

Now, let's go for a visit to the tower of Babel
(See **Genesis 11:1-9**). The whole Earth was of
one language and of one speech, which only
became a problem when they tried to make a
name for themselves and build a city that led
to Heaven. When the Lord evaluated their

thoughts and actions, He deemed it necessary and important enough to come down to Earth Himself and short-circuit their ability to communicate with one another. He also stopped the building project and caused them to scatter across the Earth. In **Genesis 11:6**, the Lord Himself testifies of strength developed from mankind coming together on one accord. But why does He disrupt the unity of these mighty people? I can hear a thunderous reply— **"Not by might, nor by power, but by my spirit, saith the Lord of hosts" (Zechariah 4:6)!**

I want to look at one more example of God's people in agreement without God's endorsement. This time, let's journey through the New Testament to the book of **Acts 4:32-35**. This was a time in the early stages of church history when believers had all things in common. No one was lacking because those who possessed items, sold their possessions or brought them to the church (the apostles) so that others could have possessions. **Acts 5:1-11** is where Ananias and Sapphira come in. There was a Christian couple who were members of the church and apparently gave to the church. They agreed to give a certain amount of their money to the church, but the church had agreed to sell their possessions and bring all of the funds together so no one would be without. This was an example of being on one accord with the Lord. Ananias and Sapphira were in their own agreement, even to the degree that they would lie about the decision that they had made concerning their own land and money. Peter reminded them individually that it was not man they had lied to, but God Himself. The Bible tells us that they both fell down and died. They were on one accord, but not with the Lord.

These examples show us the fatal consequences that we will face by uniting together outside of God's purpose. So, what can cause a group of believers to come together in the name of the Lord, yet lose focus of the same? One of the most effective enemies that separate tongue-talking, head-jerking, miracle-working Christians from one another and God is offense. That's why Jesus said, **"And blessed is he, whosoever shall not be offended in me (Matthew 11:6)**. This is a Word from the Lord that will open our eyes to clearly see the true body of Christ. Let's look at it this way—we have a choice to be offended, which gives us a choice to be blessed. I say this because offense builds a fence to create defense. So, what happens is that the offense arrives by C.O.D. (cash on delivery), and we have a choice on whether to receive it or not. Just remember, the only way to receive this offense is to pay for it!

Let's investigate what we are actually paying for. Offense comes in the form of a seed that grows up and becomes a fence. That fence is constructed through disobedience, rebellion, unbelief, doubt, schisms, unforgiveness and a hardened heart. We now find it necessary to defend ourselves from anything and everybody, including God. This is what Jesus was trying to show Peter and the other disciples. **"But he turned, and said unto Peter, Get thee behind me, Satan: thou art an offence unto me; for thou savourest not the**

things that be of God, but those that be of men" (Matthew 16:23). Jesus is telling Peter that he has been influenced by the prince of this world, because he had set his mind on human things, instead of divine things. For this reason, Jesus informed Peter that he was an offense to Him. An offense is a stumbling block, a hindrance, a stronghold, or anyone who tries to abort, disrupt, or even stop the purpose and plan of God.

Offenses make it painfully impossible to stand together as one in Christ. The bottom line is, if we harbor just one offense, we become an offense to Christ ourselves. Let us be honest and ask ourselves, "Am I an offense to Jesus?" Jesus proclaimed, **"And if a kingdom be divided against itself, that kingdom cannot stand. And if a house be divided against itself, that house cannot stand." (Mark 3:24-25).** Here's another devastating example of separation by offense. **"Then saith Jesus unto them. All ye shall be offended because of me this night: for it is written, I will smite the shepherd, and the sheep of the flock shall be**

scattered abroad" (Matthew 26:31). Jesus reminded His disciples that they would be offended because of their association with Him as it had been prophesied. From there, they went to a place called Gethsemane to pray. A short time later, they were face-to-face with Judas Iscariot and a great multitude who'd come to take Jesus away. How did the eleven offended disciples handle this situation? **"Then all the disciples forsook him and fled" (Matthew 26:56).** These are the actions of Jesus' disciples, but we are to learn from them, not to make every mistake they made. As the Apostle Paul said, **"Be ye followers of me, even as I also am of Christ" (I Corinthians 11:1).** So, let's all repent for carrying around offenses. Now we know the damages we cause within the body of Christ—from head to toe. Just remember that these offenses always come by C.O.D. It's best not to receive it, but if by chance you do because of lack of focus, don't build a fence around it. Just get rid of it, return to sender and don't worry about the postage. Jesus paid it all; all to Him, we owe. That is why

we need 2-B-1. Bless His name! I
DO...ObeDIEnce!

Chapter 18

CAN YOU STAND THE REIGN?

While preparing myself to minister concerning the resurrection of Jesus Christ, I was led to journey into an area beyond the traditional Easter message. This area is sensitive to born-again believers and non-believers alike, because it causes us to see that Jesus' rising from the dead gives all mankind an opportunity to be resurrected. **"For He Himself has said, Because I live, ye shall live also" (John 14:19).** The fear alarm sounds off when we realize that there must be a death before there is a resurrection, which means that we too must die in order to live with Him. **"It is appointed unto men once to die, but after this the judgment" (Hebrews 9:27).** The important thing is how we die, as Jesus obediently demonstrated when He boldly said to the Pharisees, **"Therefore doth my Father love me, because I lay down my life, that I may take it again. No man taketh it from me, but I lay it down myself. I have the power to lay it down, and I have the power to take it again. This commandment have I received of my Father" (John 10:17-18).** As believers, we must lay our lives down; we must take up our crosses and follow the Lord's commands. If we died to our selfish ways now, we will not have to die the second death (which means eternal separation from God to burn forever in Hell). Jesus teaches that whoever is born but once (of the flesh) shall die twice—that is, physically and eternally. He (the believer) who is born twice (of the flesh and of the Spirit) dies but once: he passes through only that physical termination of soul and body, which is called death **(John 3:3-7)**. This is the essence of the resurrection in the fullest sense of the word.

Let's look at some of the reactions God's people displayed immediately after Christ's resurrection, while the church was an infant, compared to the (supposed) more mature church of today. In the Gospel of **Luke 24:13-35**, Dr. Luke gives an account of two followers of Jesus walking to Emmaus from Jerusalem. Along the way, they sadly talked about the things that had happened to Jesus. They had an experience that we are familiar with today—if you talk about Jesus long enough, He's bound to show up! These brothers actually walked with Jesus and didn't recognize Him. Many times, we also walk with Him (spiritually) and allow circumstances around us to distort our vision to the degree where we just can't sense His presence. This is why we must walk by faith and not by sight. Fear of those circumstances will cloud our vision and distort our focus. Remember the acronym for FAITH is "Forsaking All, I Trust Him", and FEAR is "False Evidence Appearing Real." Have faith in God's promises, and you'll know that the evidence fear presents can't possibly be real. You see, we must die to ourselves to prove we believe. Christ must be allowed to reign!"

Notice how these brothers were apparently familiar with the scriptures. Just listen to Jesus. **"Then he said unto them, O fools, and slow of heart to believe all that the prophets have spoken: Ought not Christ to have suffered these things, and to enter into his glory?" (Luke 24:25-26).** The following verses show Jesus enlightening them about the things that were said by the prophets concerning Him, which caused them to hunger for more. He sat with them to eat, took the bread, blessed it, broke it and gave it to them. **"And their eyes were opened, and they knew him; and he vanished out of their sight" (Luke 24:31).** I believe their eyes of faith were opened, and they knew Him because they had communion with Him. At any rate, He blessed them spiritually by preaching the Word and physically by praying over the bread He had given them. So, through communion with Jesus —for example, worship, prayer, the preaching of and the study of the Word of God, our eyes are opened to the reality and truth of the resurrection. At this point, we find a desire, not only to proclaim Him as Savior, but to make Him our Lord. When this change occurs, there will be a burning fire in our hearts to tell others about our new-found hope, which has been revealed through the power of His resurrection. A good example of this is shown in **Luke 24:32-33,** which reads, **"And they said one to another, did not our heart burn within us, while he talked with us by the way, and while he opened to us the scriptures? And they rose up the same hour, and returned to**

Jerusalem, and found the eleven gathered together, and them that were with them." Do you see how they rose up and went to the other believers? Does this sound like the saints of today? Of course, it does! We come to the house of the Lord to preach, prophesy, shout and testify to each other until it becomes competitive. All the while, Jesus is saying, "Enter to worship; go forth to serve." This is where I believe church folks get stuck. First of all, our text tells us that while they were testifying to the disciples and the others that were with them, along came Jesus bringing peace. He then soothed their doubts and calmed their fears, proved His identity, ate and instructed them to wait in the city of Jerusalem until they would be endued with the promise of power from on High. He led them as far as Bethany, where He blessed them and was carried up into Heaven **(Luke 24:36-51)**.

In the next two verses, we can see the result of them believing that He was truly resurrected from the dead. **"And they worshipped him and returned to Jerusalem with great joy: And**

were continually in the temple, praising and blessing God. Amen" (Luke 24:52-53). They were then obedient and glad about it. Now, Jesus really was Lord and had free reign over their lives. With that reign comes vision; the vision brings provision, and provision brings power. **"But ye shall receive power, after that the Holy Ghost is come upon you; and ye shall be witnesses unto me both in Jerusalem, and in all Judea, and in Samaria and unto the uttermost part of the earth" (Acts 1:8).**

In the second chapter of Acts, you'll find Dr. Luke's account of the promises of the Holy Spirit being fulfilled, and Peter preaching a sermon that won about three thousand souls to the Lord. You could say that these brothers and sisters were in church every day and doing nothing to advance the Kingdom of God until the Day of Pentecost. And that's probably a true statement, but they were following instructions from the Lord—those instructions were to wait. We take these same passages of scripture to justify our utilizing and displaying all our time, gifts, and talents in the church building and among one another, instead of sharing with those who don't know Jesus and who are looking for an answer to their frustrated lives. This is why Jesus said, **"I am the resurrection, and the life; he that believeth in me, though he were dead, yet shall he live. And whosoever liveth and believeth in me shall never die. Believeth thou this?" (John 11:25-26).** Jesus was talking to Martha (Lazarus's sister), who had a vague understanding of the resurrection of the body at the last day. Needless to say, He wanted her to see that He Himself was that same resurrection and life. Yet, if anyone lives believing in Him, he shall never die. But I must say again, this death is what ties His Lordship to the resurrection. You see, we must die to ourselves to prove we believe. Christ must be allowed to reign! Beloved, can you stand the reign?

Let's go back to **John 10:17-18**. Jesus testified that His Father loves Him because of His obedience on the cross. He also told us how no man can take His life, but just as He had the power to lay it down, He also had the power to take it up again. After this, He confirmed that His commands are from His Father. Now, His Father is our Father, because we have faith that Jesus died on Calvary—this is relationship. No man can make me surrender my will or allow Christ to be Lord of my life. I have the power to place this life of mine in His hands or stay in control myself. But God commands me to let Christ be Lord of all—this is Lordship. That means, Christ reigns on the throne of my life. Therefore, I've already been resurrected. Hallelujah! The question is, again—Can you stand the reign? I DO...ObeDIEnce to Christ!

Chapter 19

Seven Steps to Your Inheritance (Promotion)

If you have been taking the principles of simple obedience that I have shared with you throughout this book and have begun the process of application to your everyday life, you have already said, "I DO to Christ." If this is you, then you are next in line for an elevation, but you need to be in the proper position to receive it. How do we position ourselves for promotion and elevation? Many times, we work hard to position ourselves for promotion and still blow it. We either get the promotion but find that we were not ready to maintain it or we position ourselves for consideration and then, disqualify ourselves and are bypassed. This is because our production begins to decline many times because we've began to move on to our new position that we don't actually have.

When you live for God and you're content with whatever He's already provided, then all that you need and more will be provided. Remember that statement because we're going to come back to it. Again, I say, when you live for God and you are content with whatever

He's already provided, at that point, all you need and more will be provided. **Matthew 6:33, "Seek ye first the kingdom and His righteousness and all these things shall be added unto you".**

Life is a process in itself, and there are steps that God requires us to go through as we reign victoriously throughout this life. But we must acknowledge Christ every step of the way or we are sure to get off track. **Proverbs 3:5-6, "Trust in the Lord with all thine heart and lean not to thine own understanding. In all thy ways acknowledge Him and He shall direct thy paths."**

Here are seven steps that will guarantee your inheritance in Christ, whether you're seeking a closer walk with Him, looking for a mate, a job or a career, wondering whether to make or take a business offer, debating on how far to go with an ungodly relationship, or whether you should buy or sell a home—whatever decisions that may be facing you, these seven steps will give you the direction you need to win.

Seven Steps To Your Inheritance (Promotion)
1. **Trust in the Lord and do good.**
2. **Delight yourself in the Lord.**
3. **Commit your way to the Lord.**
4. **Be still before the Lord.**
5. **Wait patiently for Him.**
6. **Fret not yourself over the one who prospers in his way.**
7. **Refrain from anger.**

Turn to **Psalm 37:3-9 (ESV)**.
1. **"Trust in the Lord, and do good; dwell in the land and befriend faithfulness."** We have plenty of reminders of this step printed on our currency! "In God, we trust!" But it means nothing if you don't actually trust Him. If you do trust Him, then you are able to do good in Him. This is where accountability comes in because, as you trust Him, He assigns people in your life who regularly demonstrate their trust in Him while assisting you to do the same. The worst thing you can do in a season of

promotion is find yourself by yourself believing that you are hearing from God.

2. **"Delight yourself in the Lord, and He will give you the desires of your heart."** This is where you learn to enjoy life just because you're in the Lord. The good, bad and the ugly! To delight yourself in the Lord means to truly find peace, contentment and fulfillment in Him. When we find joy in Him, He places joy in us—or should I say, He brings the joy with Him? In other words, because we delight in Him, He gives us what He desires for us to have. Notice, we are content in Him before we get the desires of our hearts, and we demonstrate that contentment by displaying the joy that we obtain from being in Him. We therefore become content and satisfied with being more like Christ. **1 Timothy 6:6, "Godliness with contentment is great gain."**

3. **Commit your way to the Lord; trust in Him, and He will act. 6. He will bring forth your righteousness as the light, and your justice as the noonday."** You have to make an honest

and true commitment to love what Christ loves
and hate what Christ hates.

4. **" Be still before the Lord."** You have to be
still in faith, and your faith must be in Christ.
God says to "Stand still and see the salvation of
the Lord." So, the only way we can wait on the
Lord or even wait for time is by faith. Faith
without works is dead! **"Even so faith, if it hath
not works, is dead, being alone" (James 2:17).
"But wilt thou know, O vain man, that faith
without works is dead" (James 2:20)? "For as
the body without the spirit is dead, so faith
without works is dead also" (James 2:26).**

Let me show you how easy it is to demonstrate
faith. Everyone has faith and I'll prove it. I'd like
for you to stand up and stretch, please. Now,
sit back down. When you stood up, you
exercised faith. You had faith that you could
stand. You then added works to that faith by
actually standing. You had faith that your feet
and your legs would help you to get up and
that they would hold you up. If you continued
to sit down, thinking about how you believe

you can get up and you sat there day after day believing and still did not get up, you would eventually die in your faith. Faith without works is dead! You also demonstrated faith when you sat back down, especially believing that the chair or sofa would hold you and not let your butt hit the floor.

Let's go back to **James 2:17-26 (ESV). It reads, "So also faith by itself, if it does not have works, is dead. But someone will say, "You have faith and I have works." Show me your faith apart from your works, and I will show you my faith by my works. You believe that God is one; you do well. Even the demons believe--and shudder! Do you want to be shown you foolish person, that faith apart from works is useless? Was not Abraham our father justified by works when he offered up his son Isaac on the altar? You see that faith was active along with his works, and faith was completed by his works; and the scripture was fulfilled that says, 'Abraham believed, and it was counted to him as righteousness-- and he was called a friend of God. You see that a** person is justified by works and not by faith alone. And in the same way was not also Rahab the prostitute justified by works when she received the messengers and sent them out by another way? For as the body apart from the spirit is dead, so also faith apart from works is dead."** As we continue, please keep in mind who or what we have faith in is also of the utmost importance. Our faith must be in the Lord!

5. **Wait patiently for Him. "Be still before the LORD and wait patiently for Him."** It's not good enough just to wait on the Lord, but we must wait patiently. So, when it comes to waiting on the Lord, we must always consider the principle of seed-time and harvest. In **Genesis 8:22,** the Word of God plainly says, **"While the earth remaineth, seedtime and harvest, and cold and heat, and summer and winter, and day and night shall not cease."**

What separates each of these? What separates the seed-time from the harvest? The cold temperatures from the heat? The summer from the winter? The day from the night? There is one common element that separates all of these, and that is time. Nothing can go from hot to cold without time. A season can't change from summer to winter without time. The difference between night and day is time. And the space between a seed becoming a harvest is time. As we all know, when we expect a harvest, a seed must always be sown first. But we will never enjoy a great harvest from a seed without the assistance of time. God will give us a seed attached to a harvest with time being the determining factor. So, when we talk about waiting patiently for the Lord, we're actually waiting for time to mature the seed. And somethings take more time than others. God determines the time that is necessary to accomplish all things for His purpose. So, our faith is always in God, not things or stuff or people, because all things (including the devil) exist and work together according to His purpose.

6. **"Fret not yourself over the one who prospers in his way, over the man who carries**

out evil devices." This tells us not to become envious of those who appear to have an abundance of blessings, especially those who have prospered illegally or through unrighteous mammon. Don't fret or sweat over those who are financially prospering while flaunting a lifestyle that you know is not in accordance to the will of God. It's just a matter of time—God's time!

7. **"Refrain from anger and forsake wrath! Fret not yourself; it tends only to evil. For the evil doers shall be cut off, but those who wait for the Lord shall inherit the land."** Please! Please! Please, Beloved, monitor or cut down on social media. I've learned that it is actually used by the enemy to produce anger and cause us to stir up wrath. Don't think that you are so holy that you cannot be affected by all this negativity. Social media is always packed with drama, drama and more drama! If you take it in, you can rest assured that it's gonna come back out. The question is when and how? We are also told not to fret over anger and wrath. Vocabulary.com tells us, fret comes from the

Old English word "freton",meaning, to devour like an animal. When you fret over something, it consumes your thoughts. So, this scripture basically tells us if our thoughts are consumed with drama, they will eventually produce evil. Selah!

And finally, keep your eyes on what God has already provided and is presently providing. Be sure to continually give Him thanks. As **1 Timothy 6:6 shows us, "Godliness with contentment is great gain."** Again, I say, when you live for God and you are content with whatever He's already provided, at that point, all you need and more will be provided. Jesus fed over five thousand men, women and children with two little fishes and five loaves of bread in **Matthew 14:15-21**. He simply gave thanks for what God had already provided and God supplied the need, plus an overflow!!!

So, what is it that we gain that is promised to be so great?

Well, here's the end result for your obedience to Christ due to following these seven steps in His righteousness.

Psalms 37: 9-11 "For the evil doers shall be cut off, but those who wait for the Lord shall inherit the land. In just a little while, the wicked will be no more; though you look carefully at his place, he will not be there, But the meek shall inherit the land and delight themselves in abundant peace."

Notice between **verses 9 and 11**, the Lord makes two promises for us to inherit the Earth. One gain is that the evil-doers shall be cut off. This happens immediately as we wait on the Lord and inherit the Earth. This inheritance keeps us so busy that we can't fear or focus on evil-doers because we find ourselves about our Father's business. **Verse 10** says in just a little while, the wicked will be no more. Because we are prayerful and focused on God, our attention will not be drawn to negativity.

After this, He says the meek shall inherit the Earth. So, it's not just important THAT we wait, but also HOW we wait. We must wait in a spirit of meekness and not weakness,; this causes us to delight ourselves in His abundant peace.

Recap: Here is the checklist for **The 7 Steps to your Inheritance (Promotion)**

1. **Trust in the Lord and do good. "I DO!"**
2. **Delight yourself in the Lord. "I DO!"**

3. **Commit your way to the Lord. "I DO!"**
4. **Be still before the Lord. "I DO!"**
5. **Wait patiently for Him. "I DO!"**
6. **Fret not yourself. "I DO!"**
7. **Refrain from anger. "I DO!"**

Thank you, **FATHER,** for your **HOLY SPIRIT** who teaches me on a daily basis to say, **"I DO...I Die in ObeDIEnce to CHRIST!"**

www.ingramcontent.com/pod-product-compliance
Lightning Source LLC
LaVergne TN
LVHW051054080426
835508LV00019B/1871